A Creature of Our Own Making

For Laura,
A true leader!

CAO

A Creature of Our Own Making

Reflections on Contemporary Academic Life

Gary A. Olson

SUNY PRESS

Published by State University of New York Press, Albany

For information, contact State University of New York Press, Albany, NY
www.sunypress.edu

Production by Ryan Morris
Marketing by Fran Keneston

Library of Congress Cataloging-in-Publication Data

Olson, Gary A., 1954
   A creature of our own making : reflections on contemporary academic life / Gary A. Olson.
      pages cm
   Includes index.
   ISBN 978-1-4384-4577-9 (hardcover : alk. paper)
   ISBN 978-1-4384-4578-6 (pbk. : alk. paper)
   1. Education, Higher—United States.   2. Universities and colleges—United States—Administration.   3. Educational leadership—United States.   I. Title.
   LA227.4.O57 2013
   378.73—dc23   2012015508

10 9 8 7 6 5 4 3 2 1

For Lynn,
A true intellectual and the inspiration
of many of the meditations in this volume

Contents

3
Campus Reform

4
Faculty Concerns

5

Faculty Recruitment

6

Special Topics

Introduction

A Creature of Our Own Making is a collection of fifty-eight of my monthly columns about higher education published in the *Chronicle of Higher Education* over a span of nearly six years. These short essays are meditations on many aspects of academic life, but especially on issues relevant to faculty and academic administrators. These are the original essays with only minor changes, so at times the text will refer to my tenure as dean of the College of Arts and Sciences at Illinois State University, and at other times it will refer to my position as provost at Idaho State University.

It has been my experience that we academics can be very insular, preoccupied with the intricacies of our own disciplines and thus not very cognizant of how other parts of our institutions work. Many of our colleagues could not explain what a dean does, or what a provost is, or why the academic search process works the way it does, or what academic freedom really means. Most of us go through our careers with an incomplete (and in some cases completely wrong) understanding of many aspects of academic life. These meditations attempt to shed light on the complex workings of our academic institutions.

The essays in Part 1 examine various aspects of campus culture, from treating support staff with the respect they deserve, to pitting administrators and faculty against one another in a simplistic and unproductive us-versus-them competition, to countering the kind of "gotcha" politics that is becoming increasingly—and alarmingly—more prevalent on college campuses.

Academe is often plagued by inexcusably rude and uncollegial behavior. This culture of incivility is becoming ubiquitous. All one need do is peruse discussion forums for academics and their countless blogs to see how much reasoned, intelligent discourse has eroded and is being replaced by mean-spirited name calling and finger pointing.

1

Perhaps this decline in civil discourse is related to the apotheosis of opinion. Apparently, nowadays an opinion will trump a fact, a reasoned argument, an empirically verified observation—even a treatise by an eminent scholar. An opinion is the great equalizer, and everyone has one. It silences all arguments, squelches all dialogue: That's your opinion. End of discussion.

One factor that is having a positive effect on campus culture is the movement toward increased accountability, not only in student and curricular outcomes but in budgetary transparency, disciplinary actions, and performance evaluations. Becoming genuinely accountable means being able to demonstrate that decisions derive from specific facts, not from anecdote, impression, gut feeling, personal agenda, or ideology. It entails fostering a culture of evidence within the institution.

Another subject discussed in this section is the feeling among some faculties that every important university decision should potentially be open to a faculty vote. The fact is, universities are not democracies; they are complex organizations comprising multiple constituencies all of whom contribute advice from their unique perspectives. If universities really were democracies where every important decision was subjected to a vote, they would be ungovernable.

To be effective as an academic administrator, you have to cultivate a range of skills and acquire a type of knowledge different from what it normally takes to be a successful teacher and scholar. Part 2 explores various issues relevant to the craft of academic administration, from the importance of following proper protocol, to how to deliver bad news collegially and professionally, to how to manage budget cuts strategically.

One key topic of this section is how academics find their way into administrative work; most do so by accident. An unexpected opportunity opens up, and the time is right: A department chair resigns unexpectedly, a dean suddenly accepts a position at a competing institution, a chance discussion impresses an administrator who determines to "find a place" for you. More often than not, faculty members become department heads or unit directors having had no training for the job, and must spend the first year or two learning the ropes through trial and error. There are, however, steps you can take to position yourself well for administrative work, and measures that chairs and deans might take to help you make the transition. This section examines these measures.

Also addressed is the fact that administrative decisions can often appear, at first glance, to be arbitrary or self-serving while they in fact arose out of personnel actions that compelled the administrator to observe strict confidentiality. Confidentiality over personnel issues is a burden that most administrators must bear daily. They cannot willy-nilly reveal information that could potentially damage the reputations of those faculty and staff members involved in personnel conflicts. Thankfully, however, higher education in the United States enjoys a well-developed system of protection for those accused of ethical and legal violations, even after they have been found to be culpable.

From an exploration of why rules and procedures are important, to why universities assess "chargebacks" to their own units, to the difference between a bureaucrat and an academic leader, the essays in this section explore the types of issues that will help prepare aspiring administrators to take on new positions—or simply inform anyone in the academic community about the inside workings of academe.

Universities across the nation are in constant flux as they constantly attempt to change themselves to better meet the needs of students and faculty. The essays in Part 3 deal with several areas where institutions are reforming or improving their operations. Some institutions, for example, establish in their strategic plans the goal of rising in the Carnegie classifications. This is often a worthy goal because it helps an institution focus on increasing its diversity and complexity. The Carnegie classifications, then, have become one way to measure institutional growth and progress.

Other institutions attempt to "go to the next level" by raising their research profile. Such efforts sometimes engender anxiety. and even anger among faculty who have become accustomed to the institution's traditional mission. As with actual growing pains, institutional growing pains are not easy. You may experience awkwardness and discomfort in the short term, but the end result is well worth it: greater institutional maturity and a general feeling of satisfaction about being part of an institution with higher standards and aspirations, and increased respect nationwide.

Many institutions over the last several years have undergone major reorganizations of their academic units in an effort to become more efficient, competitive, and cost-effective. These efforts also have generated a great deal of anxiety on their campuses but are leading to much more streamlined operations and, in some cases, some forward thinking departments and colleges.

Another form of streamlining that institutions are undergoing recently is curricular reform. These efforts are, first and foremost, about serving our students. It's about streamlining general-education requirements so that students can progress to graduation in a timely manner. It's about making sure that a major's requirements don't place unnecessary hurdles in students' way. And it's about trimming underproductive programs so that adequate resources can then be invested in programs with strong enrollment.

The largest and most diverse section in the book, Part 4 contains an assortment of essays on a range of topics germane to faculty and their work, from learning how to network within your discipline, to reporting faculty accomplishments accurately, to navigating the tenure and promotion system, to creating a culture of recognition and reward for faculty, staff, and students.

These essays attempt to demystify important concepts such as shared governance and academic freedom. Academic freedom, for example, is often misunderstood to be a blanket freedom covering any and all faculty speech and behavior. In reality, however, academic freedom allows faculty members to engage in research on controversial subjects (and, by extension, discuss those subjects in their classrooms) without fear of reprisal. That is, it refers specifically to academic subjects and is not a blanket protection for any and all speech in any venue. It does not protect us, for example, from other types of utterances and behavior, such as slander or libel, bullying co-workers, lying on a *curriculum vitae*, or conducting one's classes in irresponsible ways.

Similarly, shared governance is often thought to mean that the faculty have final say on some or even many decisions in the university. Shared governance, however, is not a simple matter of committee consensus or any number of other common misconceptions. "Shared" connotes two complementary and sometimes overlapping concepts: giving various groups of people a share in key decision-making processes by providing avenues to offer advice and recommendations, often through elected representation; and allowing certain groups to exercise primary (but not total) responsibility for specific areas of decision making. Shared governance, then, is a delicate balance between faculty and staff participation in planning and decision-making processes, on the one hand, and administrative accountability on the other.

Central to the future success of any academic unit is successful recruitment of first-rate faculty and staff. The essays in Part 5 focus on various aspects of recruitment. The premise of this section is that "searching" and "recruiting" are not always the same thing. The job search is a kind of courtship, and "recruiting" means wooing. Certainly, we all like to be courted, to feel wanted, so the objective of effective recruiting is to determine how to make each candidate feel desired.

This section examines the tension between ambition and careerism, the dynamics of choreographing a successful campus interview, tips for conducting high-level searches, and the role of the Internet in contemporary searches.

One key distinction made in this section is the difference between a trailing spouse and a strategic hire. All too often we as administrators fail to make the important distinction between partners who most likely would not have been hired under normal circumstances and, thus, could be a burden on an institution, and those who would be an attractive hire under any circumstances. One is a "trailing" spouse in need of "an accommodation"; the other, for lack of a more elegant phrase, is an integral part of a recruitment package.

The final section comprises meditations on miscellaneous issues in academic life, from the value and significance of commencement ceremonies, to the importance of fundraising as a way to advance the academic enterprise, to the role of campus auditors and safety officers. This section addresses the ethical use of university technology, e-mail etiquette, the role of emeritus faculty and department heads, and the proper way to evaluate administrators.

I hope you find these meditations informative and perhaps at times entertaining. They were written in the spirit of collegiality and sharing that characterizes academe at its best. The academic life is a creature of our own making; it is up to us to make the effort to understand how institutions work so that we can do our part to make that life fulfilling for our students, faculty, staff, and other members of our academic communities.

I

Campus Culture

♦

What Conspiracy?

It has become a cliché among professors to speak of power relations within the university setting in adversarial terms—as a matter of "us" (the faculty) versus "them" (by which is usually meant all administrators from the lowliest department head to the university president).

Chairs, deans, provosts, vice presidents, and presidents are lumped together in a monolithic cabal—"the administration"—all the members of which are thought to operate with lockstep consistency, presumably to advance some identical (but unspoken) agenda.

In fact, it is not unusual to hear faculty members use the language of conspiracy to characterize a campus squabble:

A colleague of mine on the West Coast once informed me that her administration had set out to "destroy" the faculty and to replace all tenure-track professors with adjuncts.

Another colleague insists that his department head and "all the other administrators" are working to turn faculty members into nothing more than 40-hour-a-week workers who soon will be required, if not to punch a time clock, at least to account for their time on the job.

A dean in the Southeast complained that the faculty in one of her departments refused to adopt a curricular change that would have revitalized the department simply because she had been the first to champion the change; the faculty claimed to be "wary of top-down management."

Such sentiments express a range of quite genuine frustrations in higher education now—a time marked by tight budgets, increased governmental and corporate interference, and a distinctly consumerist attitude on the part of students and their parents. Nonetheless, depicting campus administrators as participants in some organized conspiracy against faculty members is unproductive.

It also obscures the fact that in most cases we administrators share the exact same values and goals as faculty members; we just inhabit different roles and have very different day-to-day concerns. Most administrators hold faculty rank. Do you really think our to-do list reads: dismantle tenure, eliminate academic freedom, turn professors into automatons?

The "us versus them" rhetoric obscures the complexity of academic leadership. But it is easy to conjure up a conspiracy if you are unfamiliar with the facts—namely, that in any university of any size (and probably in every institution, regardless of size), the administration is composed of a collection of individuals each of whom represents a distinct constituency and an academic unit replete with its own specific mission, goals, and needs.

By definition, the mission, goals, and needs of an academic unit are necessarily in competition with those of other units. Each unit will compete for what it sees as its portion of the pie to support its own unique agenda. Coming to terms with that dynamic is essential to understanding academic leadership and developing a much-needed culture of trust in higher education.

Everyone understands, for example, that within a college, each department competes directly and by design with other departments for the same pool of resources. Whether it be the opportunity to hire a new faculty member, increase the operating budget, upgrade computers or scientific instruments, or expand the number of graduate assistantships, some formal process of proposal and justification usually will be put in play.

The dean's office, guided by a faculty committee, is then charged with sorting through the proposals and determining which ones to support. It is entirely appropriate for each department to be asked to make a compelling argument as to why it should receive the resources rather than some other department.

Clearly, in that scenario the department heads are hardly in collusion with one another against the faculty. In fact, their job is to serve as the principal advocates for their department's faculty, staff, and programs. Nor in that scenario are the department heads in cahoots with the dean, since the dean's job is to sort through the many worthy proposals and make the difficult choice about which of them will best advance the college's mission and goals.

In a similar vein, a dean competes directly and by design with the deans of other colleges for the same pool of resources. Well before the academic departments engage in a process of proposal and justification, the colleges will have done the same; and the provost—like the dean on the college level—will need to weigh the many worthy requests.

Should the institution put a much-needed infusion of cash into the library, invest in a new doctoral program in the college of education, support a new law review in the law school, or finance an initiative to increase SAT scores of incoming students by spending more on student recruitment?

To imagine the department heads, the deans, and the provost in a relationship of conspiracy is to fail to notice that every administrator is preoccupied with defending and advocating for his or her own unit—more often than not over and against other units and their administrators.

And the competition doesn't end (or begin) in academic affairs. The identical dynamic is in play at the vicepresidential level, too. Well before the provost opens up the formal competition for resources within academic affairs, the university president will have opened up a similar process among the vice presidents of student affairs, academic affairs, finance, advancement, and the like. Deteriorating residence halls will do battle with parking problems, campus security, aging buildings, computer systems, and athletic programs, among many other competing priorities. What's more, the president's main priority may be completely different from those of the vice presidents.

Throughout the long process of negotiation at all of those different levels, some administrators may well be ineffective advocates. We administrators do not always make the wisest decisions. Some observers may misconstrue that ineffectiveness or injudiciousness as a lack of support or, worse, as evidence of a concerted conspiracy against faculty or staff interests.

But interpreting ineffective advocacy or bad decision-making as active obstruction is to forget the academic leader's raison d'être: to serve as the chief advocate for his or her unit.

Is the process of proposal, justification, and advocacy agonistic? Yes, somewhat, but it is also healthy: Each unit within the institution should be able to justify the good things it has to offer and to make a cogent case as to why they should be supported. That process keeps us all from growing stagnant and taking our programs—academic and otherwise—for granted. It helps us keep in focus why we have devoted our lives to academe in the first place.

Administrators may well find themselves in agreement from time to time on one issue or another, but the fact is that any institution is composed of a number of self-contained (though interrelated) areas, and each leader will be busy making the best case possible for his or her area.

Far from a grand us-versus-them conspiracy, the scenario you will find without fail in every institution will be the same: Each administrator arguing vociferously and tenaciously for his or her faculty, staff, and programs. You personally will not be present each time that advocacy takes place, but you can rest assured that it is happening nonstop. It is impossible for an institution to thrive otherwise.

❖　❖　❖

Avoiding Academe's Ax Murderers

Many years ago when I directed a doctoral program in my discipline, I invited a celebrated scholar to hold a daylong "master class" for a select number of senior graduate students. He lectured for a few hours and then opened the session to questions. "Dr. Famous," one student asked, "what do we need to know to survive our first year as assistant professors?"

A notorious *enfant terrible,* our mischievous guest stunned everyone with his reply: "Remember that every department has at least one ax murderer, but you won't know in advance who it is so you'd better be on your guard."

While our guest was clearly playing to his audience for a laugh, he was also articulating what has become a lamentable fact of faculty life: Many academics regularly engage in a kind of "gotcha" politics.

The propensity to pounce ruthlessly on a politically wounded colleague is rapidly becoming a favorite spectator sport in academe. I am continually astonished by the gusto with which some faculty members will leap to attack a colleague at the slightest hint of an allegation of misconduct, even when the accused is a close friend. Or by how vigorously some department chairs will initiate proceedings against a faculty member when informal discussions might have resolved the issue in question.

Over the years, I have served on or presided over inquiry panels convened to determine whether a complaint against a professor had merit.

Invariably there would be a point in the proceedings—usually early on and before all the evidence had been considered—when some faculty member would pronounce indignantly that the accused was clearly guilty and that we should recommend the maximum penalty available. "He most certainly made an offensive remark in class; he should be suspended for at least a semester." Or, "She undoubtedly falsified her research results; she should be stripped of all future institutional support." Or, "This is clearly plagiarism; he should be fired immediately."

Although such pronouncements were always made solemnly, I could not help but detect a certain underlying glee—the kind you might find when a parent catches a child misbehaving.

When guilt is assigned before all the evidence and perspectives are heard, when the verdict is swift but premature, and when the recommended penalty is the most draconian available, we have entered the zone of gotcha politics. That zone has no room for judicious deliberation, reasoned debate, or compassion—which makes it especially out of place in an institution that has historically prided itself on championing reason, deliberation, and justice.

Undoubtedly, predatory behavior in the academic world is a convenient means of crippling or eliminating rivals. Why not accelerate your opponents' demise by advocating strenuously against them if the opportunity presents itself?

A business dean told me that one of his faculty members had become convinced that a popular associate professor regularly altered his teaching evaluations by slipping into the department late at night after students had returned their evaluation forms and removing any negative ones. The incensed colleague mounted a vigorous campaign against the associate professor, whose reputation was ruined in the process. Everyone in the college believed he was guilty. As it turned out, an extensive investigation proved conclusively that the professor was innocent; no tampering had occurred whatsoever.

The same people who are quick to ascribe guilt are often the first to violate confidentiality and fuel the engine of gossip and innuendo, which can, in effect, render irrelevant any official finding in the case. An individual may be exonerated in the end but found guilty in the popular imagination.

A favorite gambit of those who engage in such vicious politics is to enlist a student—preferably a graduate student—to do their dirty work. They will urge the student to file a complaint against a rival or spread malicious gossip. In fact, it is not uncommon to discover after some scrutiny that a student's letter of complaint against a professor was actually penned by another professor.

Gotcha politics are particularly brutal when they involve anonymity. A number of my fellow deans across the country tell me they are continually shocked by the viciousness with which some faculty members attack their chairs in end-of-year written evaluation surveys. Some evaluations contain abusive diatribes and preposterous allegations, all based on the flimsiest of evidence (or just on gossip).

University administrators regularly receive anonymous letters purporting to reveal some grievous act by a faculty member: This one has plagiarized; that one is sleeping with students; another is misusing grant money. Rarely does the anonymous revelation provide specific facts and details, much less do so in a coolly objective tone. More often it takes the form of a rant with little specificity.

The ever-increasing influence of blogs has exacerbated the problem. Blogs foster a culture of anonymity and unchecked expression without accountability. Bloggers can write whatever they want, regardless of the damage to others, and they can do so fully protected by the cloak of secrecy. In some universities, blogs dedicated to unseating the institution's president have proved quite effective. In response, some university presidents have instituted their own blogs and have made them easily accessible from the institution's Web site.

The kind of predatory politics I am describing thrive on righteous indignation and, as such, are self-serving: If you are in a position to renounce some perceived indiscretion or act of wrongdoing, then you can feel—at least to yourself—morally superior. No need to consider possible extenuating circumstances or alternate interpretations of the facts. After all, you have the high ground.

Perhaps the most extreme form of gotcha politics is the phenomenon recently dubbed "mobbing," in which a group of people collectively set out to damage or destroy a colleague's reputation. *The Chronicle of Higher Education* has reported fairly extensively on this trend and has detailed several cases in which professors and administrators have fallen prey to mob action.

We all have the right—indeed, the obligation—to point out potential misconduct when we become aware of it. Improper behavior needs to be identified and halted. But dealing with that behavior does not require ad hominem attack, abusive language, unsubstantiated allegations, or wolf-pack savagery.

It's not criticism that is in question; it's the tone and style of it.

Obviously, there is no way to legislate against gotcha politics or to prevent it by fiat. The only way to put an end to such incivility is for each of us to resolve not to be a party to such unprofessional behavior. It is in your own best interest to do so. After all, you never know when you might become the ax murderer's next target.

❖   ❖   ❖

How to Get What You Want in Academe

Professors may be among the most highly educated members of society, but when it comes to negotiating our daily professional relationships, we sometimes seem to check our intelligence at the door. Ostensibly the bastion of reasoned and collegial discourse, academe is often plagued by inexcusably rude and uncollegial behavior.

At a recent professional meeting, a department chairman described being yelled at by a faculty member disgruntled over not being assigned to teach a favorite course.

"I was flabbergasted," the chairman said. "This newly promoted associate professor hollered at me right out in the busy hallway as if I were a misbehaving child." He was especially annoyed because the complainant had chosen to adopt an adversarial tone from the outset. "The scene in the hallway was not the culmination of a long discussion or debate," the chairman said. "He simply acted out from the get-go."

It was a department chairman who did the shouting in another recent incident I know of, yelling at the dean of his graduate school because of the dean's newly imposed restrictions on doctoral-defense committees. The dean reported the incident to the chairman's academic dean, who sighed and responded, "Yes, he often behaves badly, especially when things don't go his way."

On occasion, such outbursts even escalate to the next level. I worked at a university where a fistfight once erupted between two faculty members in a department meeting. While such scuffles are rare, the fact that they happen at all illustrates the depth of passion—and, at times, ill will—that can dwell just below the surface of many a department.

An elderly professor emeritus was so disillusioned by the rancor in her former department that she told me she would not seek work as a professor today if she were a newly graduated Ph.D. "I became a professor because I wanted to live the life of the mind," she said, "not the life of a pugilist."

Students, unfortunately, are contributing to our culture of incivility. Professors and administrators report more and more incidents of students acting out in verbally abusive ways. The term "grade dispute" used to refer to a reasoned weighing of facts and evidence; now it seems to suggest a diatribe.

E-mail has exacerbated the situation. Tone is difficult to regulate in e-mail under normal circumstances, but the likelihood of producing an intemperate message rises exponentially once someone feels wronged or believes that some injustice has been perpetrated. I can't count the number of times I've witnessed individuals firing off inappropriate e-mails in a fit of pique—messages that could only be described as "screaming in print." I suspect that more often than not the authors of those immoderate messages would be shocked at the viciousness of their own prose if they could only step back and read them from the perspective of the recipient.

The culture of incivility is ubiquitous. All one need do is peruse discussion forums for academics and their countless blogs to see how much reasoned, intelligent discourse has eroded and is being replaced by mean-spirited name calling and finger pointing.

What's more, people don't seem to consider the consequences of their bad behavior. I know of a small group of faculty members who waged a vicious attack on their chairwoman over a decision she made affecting their area of study. Two weeks later, the group's ring leader petitioned the chairwoman for her "moral and financial support" of a new project he wanted to start on the campus.

"I thought I'd entered the twilight zone," she told me. "He acted as if the attack of a few weeks earlier had never happened and now we were supposed to become bosom buddies."

One serious consequence of incivility is that you can permanently damage your reputation in an institution after only a few incidents of hotheadedness. A professor I know was interested in trying his hand at administrative work, and even exhibited a fair amount of talent as a potential administrator, but officials in his institution refused to appoint him to such positions because he had developed a reputation as a "crank" after firing off multiple angry e-mail messages to his department colleagues (and copying the president) over the years.

"We will never consider him for a position of responsibility in the university," his dean told me. "He can't be trusted to demonstrate good judgment."

If you really want to accomplish your goals in the academic setting, then honey, not vinegar, is the key. No injustice, however great; no personal affront, however offensive; no decision, however wrongheaded, can justify abusive discourse—be it in print, in person, or in public.

In my experience, there's always a way to resolve a disagreement in a professional and courteous manner. Here are a few best practices:

- Assume from the start that your audience has good intentions unless proven otherwise. Doing so allows you to operate in a positive atmosphere. Adopting an adversarial approach, or assuming some conspiracy is afoot against you, only causes both sides to dig in their heels.

- Demonstrate a willingness to compromise, or at least to consider alternatives to your position. Even if, at the end of the day, you don't give ground on an issue, showing that you are willing to consider alternatives helps create a more positive and productive atmosphere.

- Avoid a win-at-all-costs logic. Are you willing to suffer the consequences of your winning the dispute at hand? Some battles are not worth losing the war over. The colleague you are opposing today may be the very person whose support you will need in the future. Calling that person an unpleasant name (however good it feels in the moment) may alienate him or her forever.

- Avoid screaming in print. By carefully monitoring your tone, especially when communicating about sensitive topics, you can prevent doing serious damage to your cause. Before you hit "send," step away from the keyboard and give yourself time to think.

- Better yet, deal with sensitive issues face to face or by phone—not by e-mail. If an issue is genuinely important to you, why jeopardize it by communicating via a medium that is notorious for creating misunderstanding and bad feeling? Direct communication shows respect for the other person at the same time that it emphasizes the importance of your request or position.

Ultimately, those tips are about protecting your reputation. It's much better to be known as diplomatic and judicious than as hostile and contentious.

I am not suggesting that we refrain from speaking out strongly, defending a position, or opposing a policy when necessary. Adversaries need to be opposed, bullies put in their place, abhorrent policies overturned, new policies championed. That is part of the daily work of academe.

And, yes, malevolent people do exist, as do conspiracies. But assuming the worst of people independent of corroborating evidence is, at best, counterproductive and, at worst, part of the problem.

Maybe you don't believe that academe should serve as a model of civility for the larger society. So consider it an issue of self-interest—civility and collegiality are key to helping you get your way in academe.

❖ ❖ ❖

That's *Your* Opinion

Not long ago, a scholar of postmodern thought taught an honors seminar on the French philosopher Michel Foucault to a class of juniors. Twenty minutes into her explanation of his theory of discourse, one of the students sneered, "Well, that's his opinion. I don't agree."

Stunned, the professor explained that, given the fact that the class had only just begun reading the philosopher's work, the first task was neither to agree nor to disagree but to understand exactly what was being argued. Agreement or disagreement was a privilege earned only after having mastered and reflected on the material.

Annoyed, the student replied, "Everyone is entitled to an opinion, and my opinion is that he is wrong."

Clearly, that undergraduate was in no position to contribute in any meaningful way to an evaluation of Foucault's thought—especially since the student had only been introduced to the material a week earlier. Yet, in one definitive statement he had dismissed the thought of one of the world's most celebrated postmodern thinkers.

The student's peremptory dismissal—"Well, that's his opinion"—is not an aberration. That assertion and the attitude it embodies have become endemic, not only in society at large but in academe. Apparently, nowadays an opinion will trump a fact, a reasoned argument, an empirically verified observation—even a treatise by an eminent scholar. An opinion is the great equalizer, and everyone has one. It silences all arguments, squelches all dialogue: That's your opinion. End of discussion.

Even faculty members and administrators are not immune from that inherently anti-intellectual attitude.

Each semester, a department head I know at a private four-year college observes classes taught by faculty members on the tenure track. The object is to help them improve their teaching and strengthen their case for tenure and promotion. In each case, the chairwoman completes an "observation checklist," recording specifics of what she observed in the classroom (for example, whether the instructor answered students' questions). Then she prepares a written evaluation based on the checklist.

In her evaluation of an inexperienced assistant professor, the chairwoman pointed to several practices that she had observed in his classroom and suggested that his teaching would improve if he discontinued them. Rather than accept—or even ponder—the well-intentioned advice, the young instructor disputed the evaluation altogether, contending that teaching is an art and everyone has his or her own style. In effect, he told her, "That's your opinion."

I also know of a college dean who was removed from office and disciplined for fiscal mismanagement. He explained to a reporter for the campus newspaper that he really hadn't done anything wrong; it was all a matter of "interpretation" of the facts. He pledged to offer the "other side" of the story sometime in the near future. The "fact" that the college was tens of thousands of dollars in the red seemed immaterial.

We seem to be witnessing the apotheosis of opinion, a trend that has grave consequences for all of us in higher education. A generation of students and others are training themselves not to become critical thinkers, not to search for evidence or support of an assertion, and not to hold themselves or others accountable for the assertions they make.

A major challenge for higher education in the years to come will be to ensure that logic, critical thinking, close reading, the scientific method, and the spirit of inquiry in general don't become lost arts—lost to the imperative of opinion.

This widespread trend affects academe in ways that are not always immediately apparent. For example, it seems reasonable to posit a connection between the increased level of litigation in academe and the insistence that everything can be reduced to an opinion.

College officials are reporting record numbers of lawsuits, many of which are frivolous. Tenure denials have become susceptible to lengthy legal challenges, even when there is a preponderance of evidence that the complainants clearly did not meet the institution's stated requirements. Some candidates for faculty positions have sued institutions because, in their opinion, they were more qualified than the individuals who had been appointed. Doctoral candidates have sued their major professors over whether their dissertations were ready for defense. And provosts are being sued over even the most minor personnel decisions, from the appointment of part-time instructors to the selection of teaching-award recipients.

As the climate in academe becomes one where opinions carry special weight, many people are finding it all too easy to challenge administrative decisions. If you believe your opinion is just as valid as the decision of the committee that recommended appointing someone other than you to a position, then you may well feel entitled to challenge the recommendation. To you that committee's decision is nothing more than another opinion.

Many academic administrators are attempting to counter the trend. More and more institutions are strengthening critical-thinking components of the general-education curriculum. Department heads and program directors are making a special effort to encourage classroom instructors to teach students how to distinguish between what is mere opinion and what the discipline considers to be a stronger truth claim.

But the glorification of opinion is not merely a curricular issue, since professors, staff members, and administrators fall prey to the same temptation. One way that administrators can help curb the ever-increasing influence of unsupported opinion is to ensure that all stakeholders understand exactly how administrative decisions are made.

Transparency and effective communication about how decisions are made will demonstrate that a formal process is in play, show how that process works, and explain why a particular decision was made. Increased transparency will not satisfy everyone, but people will find it that much harder to argue with decisions when decision-making processes are clearly articulated and available for all to scrutinize.

I am not suggesting that the world is black and white and that we should always expect to arrive at certainty in any given dispute, or that there will always be one individual who possesses the truth or who has some privileged access to "reality." Rather, I am suggesting that in academic settings (if not everywhere else) truth claims should be expected to be supported by something stronger than a "feeling" or intuition.

Even "informed opinions"—judgments based on a substantive analysis of a subject—are acceptable. What is not acceptable in academic disputes (as opposed to, say, elementary school disagreements during recess) is the facile termination of dialogue with "That's *your* opinion."

Nor am I suggesting that people should not pursue legitimate grievances against their institutions, although when we believe that all opinions are created equal, we may be tempted to forget that university officials can make perfectly reasonable decisions that don't happen to go our way.

What I am suggesting is that while the apotheosis of opinion is a broad social problem, those of us in higher education—especially in administrative posts—should take the lead in demonstrating that all opinions are decidedly not equal. That's exactly why we in the academic world exist in the first place: to sift through multifarious data and perspectives and arrive at reasoned conclusions.

But then again, that's only *my* opinion.

❖ ❖ ❖

Holding Ourselves Accountable

For at least two decades, we've spent a lot of time talking about "accountability" in higher education. As with so many things in academe, the concept means different things to different people.

What comes to mind first are the continued calls from state and federal officials for uniform standards and methods of assessing student learning. But the culture of accountability in academe involves much more than that, and has taken on the form of a movement.

The appeals for state or national standards are the most well known and have sparked considerable debate. A case in point: the call by the U.S. Department of Education's Spellings Report for specific national standards for student performance and a process for accurately measuring that performance. Most faculty members and administrators agree that establishing and maintaining standards is a healthy process. It makes sense to create metrics to judge how effective courses, programs, and institutions have been in reaching those standards.

The problem, according to many, arises when nonexperts—people from outside of the academic disciplines—are the ones responsible for devising standards for the experts within the discipline. In many states, legislatures or boards of education have imposed stringent reporting require- ments on universities in order to monitor one thing or another, and not just issues related to affordability, access to education, or assessment of student achievement.

I recall one governor who publicly proclaimed that his state's pub- lic universities were "fat" and "top heavy" with administrators. He then mandated that the universities reduce their ratio of administrators to other employees by a certain percentage—this despite the fact that the actual ratios varied widely from institution to institution.

Notwithstanding his unsophisticated attempt to solve the problem (imposing a one-size-fits-all solution with no sensitivity to the unique con- texts of different institutions), the governor nonetheless had a point. He was, in effect, suggesting that universities with bloated administrations were not being sufficiently accountable to the citizens of the state.

As public institutions, we have a responsibility to ensure that we are using public money prudently and not wastefully. Especially in tough fiscal times, taxpayers have a right to know that their money in all sectors of government is under responsible stewardship.

In fact, responsible and ethical fiscal management is a key area of the accountability movement within higher education. Early in this decade, Illinois instituted a mandatory online ethics course that all state employ- ees—including university faculty members, staff employees, and adminis- trators—must take annually. Although the course covers several topics (it varies from year to year), its main focus is on the proper management of state resources, both ethically and legally—avoiding conflicts of interest of all sorts, such as claiming reimbursements you are not entitled to; awarding contracts to friends and family members; and using department telephones, computers, and e-mail accounts to conduct personal business.

To enhance fiscal accountability, many institutions are tightening their own internal controls over the acquisition and flow of money. At my own university, for instance, we have prohibited the use of state-appropriated dollars to purchase personal (not departmental) memberships, like dues for the Rotary Club or professional organizations, and personal subscriptions to magazines and journals.

We have also strengthened our controls over the use of state money for certain types of travel as well as for food and entertainment. While grant and foundation accounts may be used for a wider range of such expendi- tures, state-appropriated dollars are closely scrutinized so that the university can always demonstrate that it is a responsible steward. Our new measures were originally triggered by the state's dire fiscal condition, but they were adopted primarily to increase fiscal accountability campuswide.

Another often-overlooked form of accountability relates to disciplinary actions. In academe's "good old boy" past, supervisors and department heads often would ignore infractions of university rules, or privately direct the transgressor to halt the offending behavior. Over the years, I have witnessed a shocking degree of laxity in such matters. I've heard department heads dismiss unethical, unprofessional, or occasionally illegal behavior because, "after all, we're all colleagues," or because, as a former chair once told me, "rocking the boat would cause more trouble than it's worth." I've seen the same negligence among supervisors toward their staff members.

In those cases, ignoring improper conduct, or simply exhorting someone privately to behave, was in lieu of what proper practice dictates: documenting the incident so that if future infractions occur, appropriate disciplinary action can be taken. Documenting improper behavior is an important form of accountability—it demonstrates that the institution takes its own rules and policies seriously and will hold all employees equally accountable for adhering to them.

Staff supervisors, department heads, and other administrators have a responsibility to hold an employee accountable; that is an inherent part of their jobs. A department chair can reprimand a faculty member, if the circumstances call for it, while still remaining a colleague. The personal should never cloud the professional in such situations.

Similarly, the annual performance evaluations of university staff members and administrators is another area in which lax habits are giving way to much more professional practices. I have known supervisors who would consistently fail to document areas of improvement in annual evaluations of their employees because they hoped to avoid conflict or wanted to be thought of as magnanimous.

That practice is unfair to the staff members because it robs them of the opportunity to improve. What's more, failing to document areas for improvement could prove awkward if the relationship were to sour, or if the employee were later to become a "problem." There would be no documented history of the staff member's actual performance.

In recent years, colleges and universities, independent of external pressure, have begun to institute sweeping measures to hold themselves and their faculty and staff members accountable in a number of areas, so much so that "increased accountability" has become a badge of pride for some colleges. That is why the Voluntary System of Assessment (VSA) program has become so popular. VSA was jointly developed by the Association of Public and Land-grant Universities and the American Association of State Colleges and Universities as a way for state institutions to demonstrate accountability both internally and to the public at large.

It is typical now for universities to display in their literature that they are committed to accountability in all areas of their operations. That is a far cry from the practices in academe only a few decades ago.

Our increased commitment to accountability has led to more deliberate, defensible, and professional decision-making. Specifically, it has highlighted the necessity of making data-driven rather than seat-of-the-pants decisions, much less ideologically driven ones. Becoming genuinely accountable means being able to demonstrate that decisions derive from specific facts, not from anecdote, impression, gut feeling, personal agenda, or ideology. It entails fostering a culture of evidence within the institution, which has led, in turn, to the increased importance of involving information-technology and institutional-research departments in key decisions.

Recently I was invited to participate on a panel of experts in information technology and institutional research about the importance of data-driven decision making in strategic planning. The consensus was that having sufficient access to the right data enables universities to make more sophisticated, fine-grained decisions and to demonstrate the rationales behind them.

Clearly, "accountability" in academe can refer to a vast array of attempts to become transparent and open in decision-making processes. Whether it is an attempt by curricular programs to illustrate that they are truly delivering what they promised, or an effort by academic departments (or entire institutions) to demonstrate that their students really are acquiring the skills and knowledge demanded by their disciplines, or measures taken by institutions to tighten their fiscal controls, the answer to "Why accountability?" is this: Because we have a responsibility as public stewards to answer for the trust we have been given.

If Universities Were Democracies

If universities were democracies, then students would always have their way, since they are invariably the largest constituent group in any institution.

Undoubtedly, grades would be abolished, classes would be optional, and the curriculum would be a matter of student choice.

In this democracy, every semester would occasion a vote of confidence (or no confidence) in every professor by the students. And the vote would be more than symbolic; it would have consequences.

Of course, if universities were democracies, then staff members would exercise considerable influence over how the institution was run, since next to students they typically comprise the largest constituent group. We might imagine a thirty-hour work week, substantial annual pay increases at the expense of other university priorities, and—almost certainly—free parking.

Then, of course, there are the alumni. Most universities these days are quite proactive in cultivating their alumni as a powerful force in making recommendations about the direction of the institution. In fact, the alumni boards of many universities have become especially influential advisory bodies helping to shape the institution's progress.

Although alumni are not usually part of the daily operation of the institution in the way that faculty, staff, and students are, they nonetheless constitute a very powerful constituency. Numerically, the alumni at any institution vastly outnumber all other constituent groups, including students. So if universities were democracies, then the alumni would have the greatest say in how things are run.

While I don't know any students, staff, or alumni who believe that universities are democracies, I have known faculty who believe just that. A business dean once told me about an incident at her institution that illustrates this belief. She had spent two years cultivating a potential donor to make a multimillion dollar gift to the college. She finally succeeded in securing a gift that would result in the college being named in honor of the wealthy donor.

When she announced the good news at a college-wide faculty meeting, she was astonished at the response of a few faculty members: they insisted that the dean submit the plan to name the college to a faculty vote. The dean was especially shocked because there was nothing controversial about the donor; he was a prominent community leader and philanthropist.

"Do you mean to tell me that we potentially might vote not to accept this huge, generous gift?" she asked the group incredulously.

One of the faculty members replied, "It's our college, and we should together make decisions like this—in a popular vote."

Needless to say, the dean declined the request to submit the plan to a vote. She told the group that she would be happy to receive input from anyone who wanted to write to her about the plan, and she certainly would take that input into consideration, but the decision itself was the responsibility of the dean, the vice president for advancement, and, ultimately, the president.

At another university, the faculty senate attempted to pressure the administration to alter a proposed response to state-imposed budget cuts. The senate objected to a number of academic program closures in the plan and preferred instead that the institution jettison its underperforming football program. The senate leadership attempted to initiate a "vote of the faculty" as to what the institution's approach to the cuts should be—this despite the fact that most faculty possessed very little information about the inner workings of the athletics program or the university's long-term planning.

It is one thing for faculty to vote on curricular change, or a new tenure policy—although even a vote on these subjects should be understood to be not the final word, but just one recommendation among others. It is quite another matter to vote on whether the institution should close a campus street to traffic in order to create a pedestrian mall, or establish a satellite campus in an adjacent town, or dip into its emergency reserve fund in order to help cover a state-mandated budget cut. These are typically decisions that derive from an institution's long-term master plan and are the purview of multiple constituencies—not just one. Yet these are all areas that faculty at some institutions have attempted to control.

What's more, in scenarios such as these, a constituency is often being asked to vote on a plan about which it typically does not have a full grasp of the facts and despite the fact that the decision affects multiple constituencies, yet invariably the voting constituency will nonetheless feel that its vote should be binding.

Perhaps the belief that all important university decisions should be subjected to a faculty vote derives from a misunderstanding of what "shared governance" is. Some faculty members believe that shared governance quite literally means that a committee or other group or the faculty as a whole votes on a proposed plan and that's it—the plan gets implemented.

A dean once told me that a faculty leader at her institution informed her that shared governance means that "the faculty run the university" and the role of administrators is to "do the daily paperwork." "He said, in all seriousness, that the faculty have the primary role of governing the university and that administrators are appointed to spare them from the more distasteful managerial labor," said the dean.

Shared governance, at least in the context of American higher education, is a product of the 1960s when colleges and universities began to liberalize many of their processes. In fact, the foundational statement on the subject, "Statement on Government of Colleges and Universities," was published in the mid 1960s by the American Association of University Professors, the American Council on Education, and the Association of Governing Boards of Universities and Colleges.

Prior to the 1960s, it was not unusual for administrators to make decisions unilaterally, without consulting faculty or other constituents. The movement toward greater shared governance was an attempt to give campus constituencies more opportunity to participate in the decision making process—not to exercise veto power through votes or other means, but to be able to provide recommendations that might help influence the final decision.

Clearly, there is a substantial difference between providing input, advice, and recommendations, on the one hand, and conducting a vote, on the other. Genuine shared governance entails the appropriate constituencies' engaging in reasoned dialogue and debate over an issue before providing recommendations to the administration through their representatives.

In contrast, subjecting every important decision to a popular vote invites constituents to weigh in on issues without having studied the facts or having heard the perspectives of other constituencies—as, presumably, their elected representatives have. It would in effect mean rule by a simple majority—mob rule, rather than true shared governance.

This is not to suggest that votes are inappropriate in the university setting. Handled professionally they can serve as a barometer of a constituency's collective feeling at the time of the vote. This should not be confused, however, with the workings of shared governance.

The fact is, universities are not democracies; they are complex organizations comprising multiple constituencies all of whom contribute advice from their unique perspectives. If universities really were democracies where every important decision was subjected to a vote, they would be ungovernable.

Creating a Culture of Respect

Back when I was new to the profession, I witnessed a senior professor shouting loudly at a departmental secretary in a busy hallway. The professor, a rather large man, stood face to face as he barked at the petite woman. He was obviously out of control, accusing her of misplacing a page of an original manuscript that she had been typing for him.

While that type of abusive tirade is, fortunately, uncommon in academe—and was just as rare then—many of us may be guilty of failing to treat administrative staff members with the full respect they deserve.

A senior scholar and prominent feminist admitted to me that as a junior faculty member, she had habitually treated office-staff members as if they were her personal assistants. "I would simply hand a test to the secretary and say, 'I'll need this by 3 this afternoon,'" she told me sheepishly. She realizes now that she must have seemed abrupt and condescending: "I didn't mean to be rude or unfriendly; I was just task-oriented."

An office manager in an academic department even told me that the faculty members had voted to exclude (she used the word "ban") staff employees from departmental meetings. Although she had worked in the department "longer than just about every single professor," she was treated as if she were not a full member—and an essential one at that, since she managed the budget and was the only one with a thorough grasp of university policies and procedures.

"I've broken in six chairmen in my time here," she said. "But only one of them ever made me feel that he appreciated all that I've done."

Those incidents illustrate a kind of inequity that continues to exist in academe despite the influence of progressive thinking about issues of socioeconomic class and cultural hierarchies: Some of us treat staff members as the second-class citizens of our departments.

Certainly times have changed, and there is considerably more sensitivity than there was a few decades ago. No longer do we think of sending the office manager out to pick up our dry cleaning. But the residue of that patronizing approach persists in some departments.

We all know faculty members and administrators who regularly chastise or snap at office workers, speak to them in a condescending tone, or treat them as if they were invisible, excluding them from departmental activities and functions. One staff member told me that some faculty members in her department—including the chair—regularly speak to her as if she were a child, even though she is older than most of them.

Why that disrespect persists is hard to determine. It's often said that administrators and faculty members seem to think they are the only ones in the university. Perhaps we get too wrapped up in our own daily work and forget those who are hired to assist us. Perhaps some academics feel that because they have earned a Ph.D., they are inherently superior to the people who work in supporting roles. Regardless, there is no excuse for treating staff members as anything less than our co-workers. And there should be zero tolerance for abusive behavior.

As a dean, I have occasionally introduced my college's office manager and budget officer to visitors by saying, "This is Sandi—she actually runs the college." Sandi would inevitably give a dismissive wave and say, "Oh, don't listen to him," but the fact is that my job would be impossible—or at least impossibly more difficult—without her. It is her vigilance that has prevented a number of potential fiscal calamities. It is her creativity that has helped us perform near miracles with scant resources. And it is her meticulous attention to detail that has helped us steer a very complex college, with a $34-million budget, through many a minefield.

Sandi is but one of a number of staff professionals who manage much of the important work of the college. There's the person who directs the general-education curriculum and deals with ceaseless complaints from students and their parents. There's the person who aids collegewide committees and supports the activities of curriculum management and program assessment. There are the many technology experts who spend their days racing from problem to problem in an effort to keep a complex infrastructure up and running. And there's the receptionist in the college office who deftly sorts through hundreds of meeting requests and manages the schedules of the dean and associate deans.

My point is that, as a workplace, an academic department is more than the sum of its faculty members. The people who fill staff roles are essential to our common endeavor. And the sad truth is that they are often poorly compensated for the amount of responsibility they have.

Treating staff members as fellow professionals extends beyond simply being civil. It means taking steps to ensure that they are full participants in the life of the department.

My college, for example, recently enacted changes to our bylaws ensuring that each of the two staff groups—civil service and administrative professionals—has representation on the College Council, our shared-governance body. We also enacted procedures that give staff employees a voice in the selection and evaluation of department heads and the creation of strategic plans.

In addition, the college sponsors regular town-hall forums with each of the staff groups. And we established staff-recognition awards that acknowledge (with a substantial monetary prize) outstanding work. Those are but a few of the kinds of measures that can be taken to give staff professionals the voice and respect they deserve as fellow members of our departments and colleges.

I know a professor who became frustrated with the "chilly," impersonal climate of her department office, so she made a habit of talking every day with staff members. She might compliment someone who did good work on a project, or ask how the kids are doing. Those simple gestures had a ripple effect as other faculty members followed suit, gradually transforming the department into a friendlier environment.

Nothing will completely inoculate the academic workplace from bad behavior, whether on the part of faculty members, administrators, or staff members themselves. But instead of complaining about the workplace we have, perhaps we should take more responsibility for creating the workplace we ought to have. We all gain when we take the time to foster a culture of professionalism and mutual respect.

A footnote: A week after the professor shouted at the secretary for losing that manuscript page, he found it in his office, stuck to the side of his desk, just out of view. I doubt he apologized.

A Culture of Openness

A fellow dean at a private university in the Northwest once told me that she routinely conceals each departmental budget from the other units in her college because she fears that revealing the numbers would lead to widespread discontent.

"If the philosophy faculty had any idea what the salaries and operating budgets actually are in biological sciences," she said, "there would be class warfare."

A provost I know at another private university claims to keep tightly under wraps the procedures he uses to determine annual faculty merit raises.

"I, of course, solicit input from the departmental committees and college deans," he said, "but I then employ a rather elaborate formula for calculating the actual performance increases. We don't release the formula because it would only cause needless quibbling over the details of the formula and thereby draw attention away from the real point: that good teaching and research will be rewarded."

Certainly, those actions are not improper or wrong per se. They are intended, I believe, to preserve harmony and avoid bad feeling. Nevertheless, such secrecy is ultimately corrosive and is likely to produce the very discontent and bitterness that those well-intentioned administrators are attempting to sidestep.

In fact, I would argue that academic administrators have a responsibility to conduct university business in as transparent and open a manner as possible, that we have an obligation not just to avoid secrecy but to actively promote a climate of openness.

The dean who conceals her departmental budgets is attempting to manage her college's affairs within the context of an inescapable academic reality: Structural inequalities are pervasive and, in effect, are a central characteristic of higher education.

But inequality does not always equate to injustice. It would be a mistake to conclude that because programs, units, or faculties don't always receive "equal" resources, some injustice necessarily exists. Different programs, units, and faculties are more or less costly for a variety of context-specific reasons.

I'm an English professor, and it would not cost much in start-up funds to get me up and running at a new college: Give me a decent computer and perhaps some money to purchase books or to travel to libraries, and I'm content. Hire a senior chemist, however, and you might need to invest $250,000 or more to equip a lab.

Although I would certainly welcome an extra quarter of a million dollars, that amount would be extraordinarily excessive for the type of research I do.

And not all chemists would need the same amount of start-up money; the amount would be dictated by the nature of their research. Multiply such disparities across colleges, and they become even more pronounced. The start-up money for a new faculty member in a college of engineering or a medical school may seem astronomical when compared to that required by our senior chemist.

And start-up money is only one of countless other differences. A sociology department with a doctoral program requires substantially greater resources than a department without one; a school of communication that operates a public television and/or radio station has considerable resource needs thanks to those stations; and a medical school's needs are multiplied when it operates an eye clinic, or a pediatric clinic, or a cancer institute—or all three.

My point is that such differences are a structural fact of campus life and that it is futile to conceal them or pretend they don't exist. A better alternative is to make those facts known far and wide—and that includes making budgets available for all to see—so that everyone understands how the university works.

The truth is that a culture of secrecy breeds mistrust and paranoia; openness and transparency lay the groundwork for understanding. As a seasoned vice president for finance once told me, "People always imagine much greater inequities than really exist. When they see the actual figures, they learn that their fears were greatly exaggerated or completely unfounded."

That is precisely what my provost friend fails to see. Concealing the formula he uses to calculate merit-based raises is most likely to cause some faculty members to imagine, ipso facto, that they were done some injustice in the process—that the colleague in the office next door fared better than should have been the case.

I would even go so far as to say that salaries themselves—of administrators as well as faculty members—should be available for all to see, as is the practice in many public institutions. Transparency in such matters, and the accountability that attaches to it, is always and only a virtue, never something to be feared.

Of course, certain aspects of academic administration must necessarily remain confidential. Administrators are obligated, for example, to protect privacy in personnel matters like disciplinary actions. It would be inappropriate for a department head, say, to divulge details of a dispute to individuals not directly involved in the case. Or for a dean to discuss confidential personnel issues involving a department head with individuals unrelated to the department or the case.

The details of personnel cases should be revealed only on a need-to-know basis so as to protect those involved. Discretion in those kinds of scenarios serves a positive purpose: protecting reputations. Secrecy in most other venues of academic governance, however, rarely serves a positive purpose.

Having said all that, I don't want to seem to suggest that injustices don't exist. Clearly they do. In a given context, a program may receive a disproportionate amount of resources, or one group or individuals may benefit unduly as a result of favoritism. But such specific injustices are different in kind from the network of structural differences I've been discussing—the fact that some individuals, programs, or units are costlier than others as a consequence of market forces and a host of other material considerations.

In fact, fostering a climate of openness and transparency is the first step to correcting the kinds of injustices that do exist. It is much easier to distinguish between genuine injustices and structural differences (and then to take measures to rectify the former) once academic budgets and other important documents and decision-making procedures are out in the sunshine for all to examine.

What's more, promoting such a climate of openness will help dissipate the us-versus-them attitude that too often plagues academe.

So my response to my fellow dean is: "You need not worry about class warfare if you do two things: Provide clearly articulated explanations of how and why structural differences exist, and make your budgets and other key documents and procedures available to all. Better to empower people with knowledge than cripple them with fear."

❖ ❖ ❖

To Party, or Not to Party

During the recent holiday season, many academic leaders found themselves in a quandary. University budgets were continuing to constrict, yet most institutions traditionally take advantage of the season by sponsoring receptions to show their appreciation of faculty and staff members.

The question on the minds of many: Was it ethical to cut programs, slash operating budgets, and require pay furloughs while spending institutional dollars on a large, festive party?

Several friends and colleagues called me to express their concern about this dilemma and to ask for advice. A provost at a public university told me he agonized over whether to give his deans the green light to hold holiday parties. Finally, he authorized the celebrations so long as they were not subsidized by state money.

"Most of my deans have nonstate funds that they can draw on for such events," he said. "Given the grim fiscal condition of our state and my university, it would be unethical, in my opinion, to expend state dollars on a party—no matter how important the event might be for morale."

A dean whose college is facing potentially steep budget cuts asked me in desperation, "Shouldn't I cancel our holiday party out of compassion for those faculty members who will likely not have their contracts renewed at the end of the year? I fear that we are sending the wrong message by having a reception in the first place, given the bad shape of the local economy."

As it turned out, she allowed the reception, and she reported that the event generated substantial goodwill and was, therefore, worth the meager investment and the risk of criticism.

Institutions have responded to this dilemma in a variety of ways.

One university leader I know simply canceled the traditional "holiday at the president's house" reception, breaking a nearly half-century-long tradition. "The cost of the event is minuscule in the great scheme of things," she told me. "But I am not about to lay off staff, facility workers, and adjunct instructors without being able to say that I saved every penny I could to preserve their jobs. To me, that's a no-brainer."

Another university president had a different philosophy. He reasoned that his institution's holiday party incurred a one-time expense of a mere $4,500—an amount that would have had a negligible effect on preserving recurring budget expenses like salaries.

"When the state demands that we return funding," he explained, "they want recurring dollars, such as salary lines. A few thousand dollars in one-time cash would not save someone from being laid off, so at least it could be invested in showing our appreciation to our dedicated employees who will survive the cuts."

A friend of mine who is the head of a midsize hospital told me that his organization faced a similar predicament last year. Budgets were tight, yet the administration wanted to honor its employees. Rather than make a snap decision, the hospital surveyed its employees and found that they would rather receive a coupon for a free frozen turkey than attend a lavish company party.

"That certainly saved our organization a lot of money," he said, "while making our employees happy."

Tough decisions are not unique to university and hospital administrators. Even Queen Elizabeth II of Britain canceled a planned holiday party at Buckingham Palace. She was said to consider it inappropriate to celebrate when the British people were experiencing a difficult economic situation.

Clearly, university administrators and others are in a conundrum here. Institutional culture can set the context for decisions about how to balance the need to recognize and reward employees with the need to be sensitive to the plight of those facing unemployment.

For example, in some departments and colleges, faculty and staff members are indifferent to institutional parties, and the turnout correspondingly light, so canceling is the obvious move. In other departments and colleges, however, the annual holiday party is a beloved tradition, so canceling to save a small pot of money may do more harm than good. I know of one college within a university in which the office staff begins planning the holiday festivities two months in advance, and people make a special effort to attend. Even the president shows up. That kind of tradition needs to be taken into consideration.

Where I stand on this: Even in the worst of times, we should make every effort to acknowledge and applaud our faculty and staff members—and it seems most appropriate to do so during the holidays. It is precisely when economic times are toughest that employees need to know that they are appreciated.

As you plan for next year's festivities and make decisions about other campus events during tough times, here are some tips:

Consolidate receptions. Within some colleges, departments have pooled their money to hold joint receptions, and within some institutions, colleges have done the same. It allows units to do more with less.

Use donated money. If your university is a public institution, a holiday reception is much more defensible if it is paid for with private dollars.

Apply common sense. This is not the time for extravagance. Hold the party, but downsize it to signal that you are sensitive to the hardships around you. During this past holiday season, many departments shortened the length of their festivities and provided far less food and beverages than in years past. Others canceled the live entertainment. More important than any of those details is that faculty and staff members have an opportunity to interact in a casual setting.

Ask for help. Obviously, if the intent of the holiday party is to recognize faculty and staff members, then you do not want to ask them to provide food and refreshments as you might at a true "potluck" event. However, some academic units supplement purchased items with home-baked goodies prepared by volunteers. In one college I know, the dean himself bakes an impressive number of cookies and brownies.

Appearances are important: We don't want to be sponsoring sumptuous parties while some employees are slated to be let go. However, we have an obligation to honor our faculty and staff members. A modest holiday reception can go a long way toward enhancing morale and is a small price to pay for much-deserved recognition.

Yes, Big Brother *Is* Watching

I worked as a consultant for a university not long ago and discovered that the hot topic there was the institution's video surveillance system. Some people expressed surprise and outrage when they discovered that the university operated an elaborate network of sophisticated cameras monitoring almost every corner of the campus. The university had no right to install that technology, critics argued, because it was an invasion of privacy, a violation of academic freedom, and possibly even unconstitutional.

I was surprised that they were surprised. For many years, universities have been employing comprehensive video surveillance to enhance campus security, and that technology has done much to reduce crime, foster a climate of safety, and even save lives.

I worked at one university where cameras caught a high-ranking administrator in the dead of night stealing a student's bicycle from a locked bike rack. After viewing the video, the administrator, whose annual salary totaled well over a third of a $1-million, resigned—all for a bike that was said to be worth only about $100.

A common crime on many campuses is the theft of purses from office staff members. Street-wise thieves—who know that many office workers store their purses in the bottom right-hand file drawer of their desks—will pass through university office buildings during the lunch hour searching for unoccupied offices. They will then snatch purses from unlocked drawers and flee campus within minutes. Campus surveillance cameras have played a major role in thwarting such thefts nationwide.

Campus officials from many institutions have told me of similar instances in which electronic surveillance has played a positive role. One midsized university's modest library has 35 cameras stationed throughout the building. "It's really for theft prevention," the college's chief information officer told me. "The very first day that we turned the cameras on somebody stole another student's laptop from her unattended bag, and we had the thief stealing it on eight different cameras. We were able to identify the person, and the student got her laptop back that same day. We're just trying to keep people honest."

Another institution was able to thwart a bicycle theft ring in which someone would ride up to a bike rack on one bike and ride away on another. Later, he would return to collect the first bike. The stolen bikes were then sold at a local flea market. Surveillance cameras caught the ring leader, and local police raided his house, finding a room full of bikes.

That university's police chief told me, "We put a lot of resources into campus safety so that when parents send their kids here they know it is going to be a safe place, and we want people in the community to know that when they come on campus to commit a crime we are going to pursue them as if they robbed a bank even though they might have only taken a bicycle."

One urban university helped solve a city-wide crime spree. A group of thieves was breaking into cars in parking facilities and stealing property from them. Nearly 80 cars were burgled, and the city police were stumped. When the thieves targeted a campus parking facility, one of its 75 cameras caught them in high definition. Case solved.

Occasionally, universities install surveillance equipment to solve specific cases. One college was experiencing a rash of muggings in one of its parking facilities, so the campus increased the number and visibility of surveillance cameras; the crimes stopped immediately thereafter.

At another institution, someone was stealing women's underwear from a dorm laundry room. Campus security installed a hidden camera and planted some leopard-print panties complete with special markings. When the police, using the footage, arrested the towering 250-pound thief, he was wearing a pair of the stolen underwear.

At yet another college, campus officials discovered that theater majors were engaging in sexual acts on the catwalks high above the stage in the performing arts theater—during performances. (Students referred to it as the Mile High Club.) The officials installed cameras and were able to identify the culprits.

"We weren't trying to be voyeuristic," the chief security officer told me. "We were trying to prevent a disaster. Can you imagine a standing-room-only crowd for a Shakespeare play and suddenly a couple plunges from the rafters to the stage below?"

Video is used not only to solve crimes but to prevent vandalism and to monitor equipment that might be sensitive to the institution, such as generators or electrical equipment. Most colleges experience a spike in vandalism early in the fall semester when new first-year students arrive on the campus. After the first few perpetrators are caught and made to pay restitution, the vandalism typically drops off.

"We usually don't take students to court because that would really hurt them, but we do make them pay restitution and that hurts their pocket books," said one university official. "We tell them that if they go to the cashier's office and pay restitution by a certain date we won't press charges."

Typically, cameras are placed at building entrances and exits, stairwells, lobbies, parking areas, "at-risk" sites (where someone might be easily attacked), and any location where money changes hands. Key cameras can be monitored in real time, while the footage from others is simply recorded and stored digitally on servers, to be retrieved when a problem arises.

Many colleges and universities are in the process of upgrading their surveillance to Web-based, high-definition, digital equipment that allows the appropriate officials to access all campus cameras from a laptop wherever Internet access is available. Often, institutions then share access to the cameras with local police so that they, too, can monitor the footage when necessary.

That collaboration with local police is especially useful in "active shooter" situations—that is, when armed assailants are in the process of attacking people or threatening to. A Web-based system allows first-responders to view what is happening in real time right from their patrol cars as they approach the scene, vastly reducing the response time to a potential massacre.

Obviously, campus officials must exercise good judgment in how they employ video surveillance. Best practice, and common sense, dictates that cameras not be located in restrooms, locker rooms, or residence halls—only in public areas. Most institutions archive the footage for a specific time period (six months in many cases) and then destroy it. The vast majority of all video footage recorded on a campus is never viewed; it is only viewed when a problem arises.

And campus security must take measures to maintain the chain of custody of all recorded video in the event that a case does enter the legal system. An official may be asked to swear under oath that only certain people had physical access to the servers containing the recorded evidence and to certify that the recording is an official record of the institution.

Camera surveillance is only one component of a comprehensive campus security system, which might include, for example, card access to buildings. Card keys are not only convenient, but the card readers record the comings and goings of everyone, which can place someone at the scene of a crime or rule him or her out altogether. Even the campus' wireless access points play a role, in that the system can track the whereabouts of devices. "If someone steals your iPad," explained one chief information officer, "I can electronically watch that stolen item moving down the hallway and then down a stairwell and then across the quad."

Campus surveillance has resulted in some unintended consequences. The Clery Act of 1990 requires that colleges report annually on all crimes on their campuses, and those statistics allow students and parents (and faculty members, for that matter) to make informed decisions about whether to attend a given institution. Some institutions experienced a sharp increase in the number of on-campus arrests for crimes such as vandalism, assault, and drug possession after increasing their video surveillance, and as a result their crime ratings would be artificially inflated compared to campuses with less surveillance. Nevertheless, the advantage of solving or controlling campus crime far outweighs that public-relations drawback.

So while some on campuses may characterize video surveillance as an Orwellian Big Brother scenario, the technology is deterring campus crime, solving those crimes that do occur, making our campuses safe to traverse at night, and even, occasionally, saving lives. So, yes, Big Brother is watching—and it's a good thing, too.

2

The Craft of Administration

◆

How to Join the Dark Side

The original *Star Wars* film was not even a year old when the now-clichéd retort had already begun to circulate through academe: After accepting an appointment as department chair, your colleagues would stop you in the hallway and ask ominously, "So, you've decided to join the Dark Side?"

I was tempted to repeat that retort recently to a freshly tenured associate professor who had asked me how one "gets into" academic administration. She was fascinated by the possibility of pursuing administrative work, but the process seemed impenetrable. Her question is a good one, since most institutions provide little or no formal preparation for faculty members who wish to pursue administrative work. As a result, many think of it as remote, abstract, and out of reach, if not downright undesirable.

This young professor may well have an advantage over many of us who rose through the faculty ranks. Despite being early in her career, she has already begun to consider the possibility of administrative work and is beginning to formulate a game plan. That is not the case for most would-be administrators.

A successful university president I know could serve as a role model in that she carefully mapped out her career trajectory quite early in her career. While still an advanced associate professor, she devised a long-term plan: By the age of 45, she would be a dean at a research university; by 50, she would be a provost; by 54, a president. She was uncannily prescient: As if on cue, she took over the reins of one of the nation's largest public research universities shortly after her 54th birthday.

Such a career trajectory is more the exception than the rule. Most academics find their way into administrative work by accident. An unexpected opportunity opens up, and the time is right: A department chair resigns unexpectedly, a dean suddenly accepts a position at a competing institution, a chance discussion impresses an administrator who determines to "find a place" for you.

To be an effective administrator, you need to cultivate a knowledge base and a set of skills quite different from those acquired in the normal course of faculty life. You need facility with academic budgets, knowledge of legal issues in academic settings, deftness in handling conflicts, ability to cultivate and steward donors, familiarity with the workings of the state legislature, a thorough understanding of how other areas of the institution work and intersect with your own. More than anything, you need to be able to think outside of the discipline in which you were trained—perhaps one of the toughest hurdles for many Ph.D.'s to overcome.

But there are steps you can take to position yourself well for administrative work, and measures that chairs and deans might take to help you make the transition.

Serving on a universitywide tenure committee, for example, can help you develop a broad appreciation of the differences among disciplines: Faculty members in fields with a heavy clinical load, for example, would be expected to spend many hours a week in clinical practice and supervision, and therefore, might not produce the same volume of published research as would someone from a nonclinical field. Certain humanities disciplines might place a high priority on producing books, unlike in the natural sciences. Developing an understanding of such differences will help you as an administrator deal fairly and effectively with diverse constituents.

Another way to gain a broad perspective of an institution is to serve on a panel charged with devising or updating the strategic plan. A well-conducted planning process will assess and account for academic goals and needs. It will also scrutinize other campus priorities, such as those outlined in the university's master plan, which details the projected evolution of the physical plant (which buildings to phase out, whether to permanently close a street on campus and transform it into a green pedestrian thoroughfare, etc.).

Of course, a time-honored step on the path to administrative work is to serve as chair of the faculty senate. That position typically affords you direct and frequent access to key administrators, as well as an insider's view of crucial issues and developments. Sometimes the head of the faculty senate serves on the president's cabinet or advisory committee. Many senate heads have gone on to become successful academic administrators, thanks in part to that experience.

Perhaps the biggest stumbling block to becoming an administrator for some faculty members is their own reputations. In attempting to be passionate advocates for this or that cause, they vigorously argue for their position but forget to do so with temperance, diplomacy, respect, and civility. As a result, they run the risk of coming across as troublemakers or cranks rather than as reformers or ardent advocates. Once you acquire a reputation as an agitator or a loose cannon, many decision makers are reluctant to entrust you with administrative responsibilities. The key to offering constructive criticism is in the execution.

While serving on campus committees can be excellent preparation for a budding administrator, more-formal opportunities are also available. Various professional associations offer a whole range of books, seminars, Webinars, and conferences on various aspects of academic administration, although most such opportunities come with a price tag. An entrepreneurial faculty member might find a way to persuade a department head or dean to foot the bill under professional development. (And, of course, most schools of education offer courses and degrees in higher-education administration.)

Ironically, many faculty members become aware of professional-development opportunities offered by organizations like the American Council on Education only *after* they have been appointed to administrative posts. Then, desperate for good practical advice, they scramble to sign up for a workshop or two. It would be much better to attend introductory seminars or Webinars as soon as you have decided to pursue the administrative-career track, so that you are well prepared when your time comes to be appointed. More often than not, however, faculty members become department heads or unit directors having had no training for the job, and must spend the first year or two learning the ropes through trial and error.

Deans and provosts could easily reverse that trend. As dean at another university, I sponsored a mentorship program for faculty members in their first two years. We emphasized the importance of building professional relationships with colleagues and administrators from outside their departments. We wanted them to develop a broad perspective about the university and how it worked. It is precisely that broad perspective (as well as the professional relationships) that will eventually be so crucial to an aspiring administrator.

In addition, we created a one-time session for newly tenured faculty members in which we discussed how their careers objectives and priorities might change now that they had tenure. We stressed that they now had the luxury of easing up a bit on their research and participating more fully in the governance of the institution through the faculty senate and its various committees.

Many colleges sponsor an "administrative fellows program." It often takes the form of a competitive internship award in which a faculty member can earn the opportunity to participate in a semester-long internship in the office of the dean, provost, or president. Internships of that type are valuable because they afford direct experience in administrative planning and practices. Other institutions sponsor in-house workshops for new department heads. Participants read and discuss literature on best practices, listen to guest speakers, and review and discuss case studies. Those kinds of workshops prepare neophyte chairs not only for their new positions but also for more-advanced administrative posts in the future.

Those are only a few steps that faculty members can take to prepare for administrative appointments, and that institutions can take to support aspiring administrators. The important point is that if you're going to play Darth Vader, you might as well know in advance what you're getting into.

The Importance of Protocol

University presidents often complain that academe has lost its sense of proper protocol. Stories abound of students disgruntled over a bad grade or faculty members disenchanted with a departmental policy who leap over several layers of authority to take their concerns directly to the provost or the president—or even, at times, to a university trustee.

People seem to have no qualms about approaching any university official whom they believe can bring about a desired result, regardless of the institution's explicit procedure for addressing such concerns. I know of one incident in which an undergraduate accounting major complained directly to the provost that her department refused to offer a required class that she needed at a time convenient for her schedule. She demanded that he immediately open another section of the class.

In similar fashion, an associate professor of engineering e-mailed his university's president to complain that his department failed to honor his request to teach a favorite graduate course. He pleaded for presidential intercession.

In those and countless other scenarios, the complainant chose not to follow the accepted procedure and instead opted to go over the heads of one or more responsible officials.

The loss of professional etiquette is often attributed to a culture of entitlement that seems to characterize not only academe but contemporary society as a whole. Personal desires and aspirations seem to trump any concern for the greater good.

Whether that sense of entitlement is a result of a consumerist society encroaching on the rarefied terrain of academe, or of baby-boomers' pampering of their children, the fact remains that the time-honored, orderly, and collegial way of dealing with issues in academe seems to be deteriorating.

E-mail has contributed to the problem. The e-mail addresses of even the highest-ranking officials are readily accessible, and so many individuals feel free to communicate directly with someone at the top of an organization rather than with the appropriate accountable officer.

And the immediacy of electronic communication militates against an environment of carefully reasoned dialogue. E-mail invites people to fire off messages in exasperation or frustration without first calmly considering the consequences. As a result, university officials find themselves dealing on a daily basis with increasingly more inappropriate petitions.

Following proper protocol is a sign of respect both for academe's system of etiquette and for the individuals involved. Protocol—not to mention common sense—dictates that students who are concerned about a grade should first communicate with their instructor. If, after attempting to resolve the issue that way, students still believe some wrong has been perpetrated, then—and only then—should they pursue the next step in whatever procedure is in play at the institution.

The student owes the instructor the courtesy of allowing him or her to determine whether a mistake was made and, if not, to explain why the grade was justified. Rushing off to complain to a department head—or, worse, to a dean, provost, or president—deprives the instructor of the ability to address the issue before it grows unnecessarily into a larger problem.

In fact, complaining first to a higher authority seems to imply that the instructor ipso facto has done some wrong before he or she has been afforded the opportunity to set the record straight.

Protocol works in an identical fashion at other levels in academe. When a faculty member chooses to bring a departmental issue to the dean rather than first attempting to resolve it with the department head or colleagues—or when a department chair chooses to skip over the dean and bring an issue first to the provost—those actions rob the accountable officer of the ability (and responsibility) to address the problem.

If, as dean, I chose to present an academic-affairs issue directly to the president rather than to the provost, it would not only be an affront to the provost, it would tag me in the eyes of others as someone who either didn't understand how the rules work or was willfully setting aside the rules simply because I wished the issue to be dealt with more expeditiously than it might have been otherwise.

But if your true objective is resolution (as opposed to, say, making someone look bad to a superior), then skipping levels of authority is a distinctly inefficient way to proceed.

For example, what typically happens when a complaint arrives on the president's desk is that it is forwarded down the chain until it reaches the level where it should have been addressed in the first place. Sending a complaint about a grade to the president doesn't produce a faster result than dealing with it in the department because the president will ask the provost to deal with the issue; the provost will, in turn, ask the dean to look into the case; the dean will then direct the department head to investigate.

Clearly, it would have been much more efficient to begin at the departmental level in the first place.

Violating professional etiquette can result in significant unwelcome consequences. When you knowingly go around someone, you, in effect, are saying, "I'm more important than the process." At the very least, it makes you appear selfish. Even worse, leaving someone out of the loop may cause that person to believe you are hostile, a perception certain to create lasting ill will.

In a more general sense, ignoring protocol creates an atmosphere of suspicion that fuels an us-versus-them climate.

Perhaps some people confuse academe's increasing commitment to transparency and openness with an invitation to approach any official likely to get them what they want. Transparency and openness mean that an administration is committed to decision making in the sunshine, that the mechanisms of decision making are clear, and that the records of such decisions are readily available.

Similarly, an administrator who advertises an open-door policy is not inviting everyone to violate protocol. That policy merely signals that an administrator is available to be called upon within the institution's usual procedures for conducting business. It doesn't mean anyone can walk into an official's office and demand action.

In short, those who knowingly ignore protocol abuse the system, insult those involved, and risk tarnishing their own reputation.

And proper protocol works in both directions. If, as dean, I wished to invite a faculty member in the School of Communication to help the college produce a video celebrating its anniversary, professional courtesy would dictate that I first inform the faculty member's department head. The chair would surely feel blindsided to learn of the project through hallway gossip.

Some administrators make it a habit, whenever they communicate with someone below their level of authority, to "copy" the recipient's supervisor. That practice ensures that the right people are always in the loop. It's not just a matter of professional courtesy; it's a professional responsibility.

I don't mean to suggest that no one should ever skip a level of authority. If you have a legitimate personal complaint against the person you report to, then it is clearly fitting to bring the issue to the next level. Or if the process on one level has been exhausted, it might be time to move to the next level. Those are the natural and appropriate courses of action, and that is precisely what it means to follow proper protocol.

And I don't mean to suggest that responsibility lies only with those who attempt to circumvent the process. If administrators themselves would consistently respect protocol, they could avoid the many attempts to get them to intervene inappropriately. But, too often, administrators are tempted to try to "fix" a problem brought to their attention rather than refer the petitioner to the proper level.

The more we as administrators give in to such temptations, the more we invite others to attempt end runs.

Arguing that we should adhere to academe's system of professional etiquette is not a defense of tradition for tradition's sake. It is an appeal to act responsibly—to avoid falling prey to the immediacy of e-mail, to instant gratification, to the temptation to damage someone's reputation, or to any of the other motives that cause us to violate academic propriety.

As in the world beyond academe, good etiquette promotes good will; its absence fosters resentment and discontent.

❖ ❖ ❖

The Administrator as Magician

My college has just developed a "partner accommodations policy" that outlines how various offices will aid, "whenever possible, the hiring of qualified partners and spouses of candidates who are being recruited or offered a retention package." The college pledges to work with academic departments and other campus units to assist partners and spouses in their search for employment, and it outlines the concrete steps that college officials will take toward that end.

A faculty committee had recommended we develop the policy to aid in recruitment, and we posted an early draft on the college Web site to give everyone a chance to comment.

After we revised and adopted the policy, a faculty member scheduled an appointment with me to discuss the measure. He was unhappy because, in his words, the policy has no teeth. He felt that the college should instead establish a partner-accommodations fund of $1-milllion so that we could simply hire qualified spouses or partners when the occasion arose.

"And where would we get these recurring, not temporary, funds?" I asked.

He replied that he was certain we could cover the expense. The implication? We were just being obstinate in not allocating the money to what everyone agreed was a worthy cause.

At a professional conference recently, a provost told me a similar story. A junior faculty member approached her with a formal proposal asking the university to make a long-term investment in a program in alternative-fuels research because such research was clearly the wave of the future (and also the petitioner's area of expertise).

The proposal elaborated a long list of demands, including new personnel and sophisticated scientific instrumentation. "I couldn't believe my ears," the provost told me. "He actually believed I could snap my fingers and thereby authorize the hiring of four or five new faculty members, not to mention equipping several very costly labs." The petitioner seemed somewhat piqued, she said, when she explained that if she had such resources, she would already have made the very investment he was proposing.

I heard yet another story about a distinguished chemist who arrived unexpectedly at his department head's office and announced that he had become so famous (and therefore so valuable to the institution) that he would now require a research lab double the size of his current workspace. Nonplused, the chair pointed out that the department's two newest faculty members had yet to be assigned adequate lab space. "I'm sure you can find me the space," the chemist replied. "This institution will not want to lose me."

Clearly, all three individuals feel they are being deprived of essential resources and that their institution is standing in the way of what are unmistakably (from their perspective) the right actions. A generous interpretation of that dynamic is that they somehow perceive administrators to be magicians who, given the right incantation, can make money materialize out of thin air. A less generous reading is that they imagine administrators to be sadistic or arbitrary parental figures: "Because I said so; that's why!"

The notion that administrators routinely withhold goodies—dollars, faculty lines, facility space—out of some irrational parsimoniousness seems counterintuitive to me. It is in every administrator's best interest to make a genuine and sustained effort to help professors and programs succeed; to retain an outstanding faculty member, and even to appoint a qualified spouse, if possible; to create a cutting-edge research program that distinguishes the institution; and to keep faculty members happy, especially senior scientists who may, in fact, be recruited by competitors.

I would love to be able to finance every worthy project that crosses my desk—and there are many of them. I would like to ensure that every faculty and staff member had the most up-to-date equipment, the most generous course load, and the ideal office or lab, complete with a view of the quad. And, of course, I would like to ensure that everyone is paid a wage that they themselves would agree is appropriate.

After all, who wouldn't want to play Santa Claus all year round?

The sad reality is that no administrator can support everything, regardless of how well endowed the institution. Like it or not, higher education is characterized by an economy of scarcity. We are all constantly competing for what seems to be ever-dwindling resources—especially those of us in public institutions. Neither Santa nor magician, the typical academic administrator is simply trying to do the best he or she can with the limited resources available.

What seems to get lost in the often fraught encounters between administrators and petitioning faculty members is that, most of the time, both sides share the same goals. The disconnect is not between a good proposal and an intransigent administrator; it's between a good proposal and fiscal realities. We are all engaged in a common endeavor, under less-than-ideal circumstances.

The fact that some administrators act in arbitrary, less-than-altruistic ways or support only their own pet projects does not mean that administration in general operates that way.

Most of the administrators I know would much prefer to play Santa over Scrooge. In the final analysis, "administrator as magician" is a more fitting metaphor than "administrator as cruel parent."

As presidents, provosts, deans, or chairs, we all keep searching for those magic words that will make everything right. Until I stumble upon that perfect incantation, however, I am going to continue to make every effort to support as many of the fine projects and faculty members as I can given the constraints imposed on me. Who could possibly ask for more?

The Burden of Confidentiality

Over the years, I've observed countless department heads struggle with faculty members over administrative decisions that appeared, at first glance, to be arbitrary or self-serving. But often, those decisions arose out of personnel actions that compelled the department heads to observe strict confidentiality. The chairs were powerless in defending against criticism because to do so would reveal that a personnel action was at the root of the decision. That very revelation would likely signal who was involved, thereby violating confidentiality even without divulging details.

That scenario presents a conundrum for any administrator, but especially one committed to transparency and openness: How do you justify your silence or lack of a detailed explanation about a decision, especially when you have been espousing respect for "process" and shared governance?

One department head I know suffered incalculable damage to her administration when she removed a popular faculty member from the post of graduate-studies director and replaced him with a less-influential junior colleague. A sizable faction in the department accused the chair of cronyism because the outgoing director did not have as clear a political allegiance to the department head as did his replacement.

Absent the facts, the chair seemed to be acting in a purely self-interested fashion and without concern for the department's collective will.

The behind-the-scenes story revealed a much-different reality. The graduate director had, for a half decade, engaged in a pattern of serious misconduct. He had used his power and influence to alter the official grades of students he favored, overriding the legitimate grades their professors had given them. He further violated university regulations by arbitrarily and unilaterally waiving required courses for certain students, and he manipulated the composition of dissertation committees to benefit certain students.

The chair learned about those abuses of power from a confidential complaint filed by a politically disinterested but nonetheless concerned doctoral student. A discreet investigation confirmed the extent of the misconduct. The department head had no recourse but to remove the director, immediately. Of course, the ousted director suffered other repercussions as well: The dean issued a stern, confidential letter of reprimand stipulating that any further incidents of misconduct could potentially result in permanent dismissal.

All of those personnel actions—the initial complaint, the investigation, the finding of misconduct, the official penalties (including the formal reprimand and removal from office)—were conducted in private so as to protect the reputations of all concerned, both the innocent and the perpetrator. Those facts did not need to circulate; the situation had been properly investigated and remedied.

When the department head first announced that the graduate director would be replaced, a large number of faculty members in the department complained vociferously that they had not been consulted. They accused the chair of acting unilaterally, with some (unstated) personal agenda. The irony was that university policy stipulated, as is the case at most institutions, that the graduate director served "at the pleasure of the department head." Technically, the department head did not even need an "acceptable" reason to replace the director, although, politically, it's always good practice to consult all of the affected parties.

But because the department head was ethically prohibited from revealing confidential personnel information, she was powerless to explain her actions, and, as a consequence, she remained vulnerable to unfair and misguided criticism. She told me that maintaining her silence was one of the most difficult and painful things she had ever done.

"I could have shut them all up by telling them the truth," she said. "But that would have been deeply unethical."

A dean in a college of applied technology experienced a similar incident. He "nonreappointed" a tenure-track faculty member who was halfway through his third year as a new assistant professor. The young faculty member was suddenly and mysteriously removed midsemester from all teaching and student-advising duties. By semester's end, he had quietly vanished from the university.

Some faculty members complained that the dean "had it in for" the faculty member and accused him of "heavy handedness." Some even went so far as to suggest that, because the released faculty member was Hispanic, the dean was motivated by racism.

In fact, the young assistant professor had proven to be a sexual predator and had coerced several undergraduates into sexual liaisons. One of the students eventually reported the professor to the department head, who immediately consulted with the dean. The department head and dean were able to establish conclusively that the professor was using grades as a weapon to have his way with several students.

Clearly, those were facts that no administrator could ethically reveal to colleagues, even "in confidence." The dean in this case respected confidentiality, even though a majority of his faculty members assumed that he had acted with less-than-noble motives. The dean's reputation in the college was severely damaged because he appeared to be a bully, yet the truth was that he had taken decisive measures to protect students from the true bully.

Confidentiality over personnel issues is a burden that most administrators must bear every day. Academic culture is one of fair play and ethical treatment of personnel. Were that not so, administrators could willy-nilly reveal information that could potentially damage the reputations of those faculty and staff members involved in personnel conflicts. Thankfully, however, higher education in the United States enjoys a well-developed system of protection for those accused of ethical and legal violations, even after they have been found to be culpable.

Of course, an institution will feel no compunction to publicize wrongdoing once a case rises to a certain level of seriousness and criminality. It is not uncommon for an institution's media-relations department to issue a news release announcing that a certain professor or administrator has been suspended for alleged embezzlement and that the local police have assumed responsibility for the case. But the typical case that most administrators deal with is more minor yet nonetheless consequential. And in such cases, the processes of investigation and adjudication occur in private and with respect for the privacy of all parties.

Obviously, an unscrupulous administrator could abuse the system by invoking the excuse of a "personnel decision" in order to conceal arbitrary or self-serving decisions, but I suspect such cases are rare. (And, besides, how often can you make that invocation before losing credibility?) More frequent is the daily torrent of legitimate personnel disputes that we all must sort through and attempt to adjudicate.

Perhaps what is needed here, more than anything, is to balance a healthy skepticism with a faith in the good intentions of those charged with leading our departments and colleges. I have great admiration for the innumerable academic leaders who, at great cost to their own careers and relationships, protected the confidentiality of others because it was the right thing to do. They fell on their swords for the very principles we hold so dear in academe: fairness, due process, and respect for privacy. Confidentiality in some of those cases was nearly an unbearable burden.

❖ ❖ ❖

Avoiding the Hunker-Down Strategy

At a professional meeting recently, I was chatting during a coffee break with a group of deans when the conversation turned to a subject they found troubling: departments that make bad, clearly inappropriate decisions and then defend those indefensible positions with vigor.

One of the most common examples is the department that votes to recommend tenure for a colleague whose case is indisputably weak— someone whose teaching is consistently rated below average, whose research productivity is practically nonexistent, and who has done minimal service over the past five years.

Frustrated with that recurring phenomenon, one of the deans had taken a trusted department chair aside and inquired as to how he could possibly have supported such a weak case. After some cajoling, the dean extracted from the department head an awkward admission: "Well, we were trying to protect the department's resources from erosion. We just don't trust upper administration."

What he meant was that if the department were to lose a faculty line, even temporarily, the department's budget would be reduced by the amount of money for that position. And since, in most institutions, the allocation of new money is typically based on a percentage of a department's overall budget, the department could stand to lose money if it lost a faculty line. In addition, in most institutions there is no guarantee that a department will ever see a vacated line again; it could well be redistributed to a department in greater need. Or, more likely, the department may eventually get the position back, but at a greatly reduced level of funding: A position slot that once contained enough money to finance a highly paid full professor might now contain only enough for a new assistant professor.

In effect, that department chair sheepishly admitted that his department had colluded to lower standards and overlook personnel problems to "protect" his department's position within the institution. The facts—in this case, the job performance of a faculty member—were of less consequence than the larger purpose of protecting and preserving the home unit from a perceived threat: the central administration.

Deans see many examples of that same phenomenon. One dean told of a department in which the faculty members tenaciously defended a colleague who had been proven guilty of serious wrongdoing, including embezzlement. The department members dismissed factual evidence arising from a formal investigation and insisted that the administration was attempting to "frame" their colleague.

Another dean related a similar story about a faculty member who was accused of sexual misconduct with a student. After the student filed a formal complaint, the incident was investigated, first by a dean's panel and later by a universitywide committee. Citing "overwhelming evidence" presented by both committees, the university dismissed the professor. Ignoring that evidence and the work of the two committees, his colleagues rallied around him and campaigned to exonerate him.

I have personal knowledge of one department where, for many years, its leaders turned a blind eye to a climate in which faculty members regularly provided false or exaggerated information about their accomplishments on the annual reporting form that they were required to submit. The form was used to make decisions about merit-pay increases and recognition awards, and also to assess a department's scholarly productivity (number of articles published, grants won, and so on).

That wasn't a case of incompetence, or lack of due diligence. It was a deliberate unwillingness to judge colleagues and find them wanting. Why? Again, because the department profited when its faculty members were all judged to be superior. Like the fictional Lake Wobegone, everyone was judged to be above average.

A friend of mine briefly served as chair of that department, and I asked her outright what accounted for its culture of protection and isolationism. She replied: "We want the administration to believe we are one of the best departments in our discipline in the nation. That way, we will continue to receive the funding we deserve. Why should we give them evidence to the contrary? That would be crazy."

That is, faculty members deliberately misrepresented the department in an effort to trick the institution's central administrators into treating it better than perhaps it deserved.

I call that strategy the "hunker-down approach"—it's us (our department or our program) against the rest of the university, so let's take whatever measures necessary to promote ourselves and minimize any negative press. I've often been amused at how some institutions have bragged that one of their programs is "the best in the country" or is "ranked in the top 10 in the nation." In many instances, such claims are made despite the lack of an actual ranking system; they are simply asserted by those in the program and then repeated by those charged with advertising the institution's strengths.

For me, the added irony of the discussion with deans that day was that they are often guilty of the same behavior: jealously defending college-level decisions that have little merit, or inflating their college's rankings because they hope to protect their budgets and their position relative to other colleges in the institution.

Certainly, part of the job of any dean, department head, or program director is to promote and advocate for one's unit. But there is a huge difference between honest advocacy and misrepresentation. When a department intentionally supports a weak tenure case, defends a colleague found to be guilty of criminal activity, permits the doctoring of credentials, or inflates the rankings of its programs—all to benefit monetarily—then professionalism has left the premises. In those cases, rather than relying on facts and evidence, departments chose to create and perpetuate a fiction.

The real problem that underlies all of those examples is the mistaken assumption—and it is widespread in many departments—that somehow the institution's central administration exists in perpetual opposition to individual departments or programs. The "us-versus-them" attitude is extremely destructive, and it even strikes me as bizarre, yet I have heard it repeated in many universities for decades.

In reality, central administration exists, in large part, to support all of an institution's many programs and departments. At times, difficult decisions need to be made—a program eliminated, a faculty line reallocated to another department, two departments or programs merged into one. But such decisions are typically not made to punish or be detrimental to a department; they are usually made for other reasons, such as increasing efficiency or responding to a budget cut.

Let's not confuse strategic decision making with being "against" a department. In fact, it is in the best interest of any administration that each and every one of its programs thrives. Working to thwart departments is working against yourself.

❖ ❖ ❖

Resist the Rush to Judgment in Disputes

A senior professor scheduled a meeting with his dean to complain about his department chairwoman. He presented a litany of grievances that, in aggregate, suggested a serious case of harassment and retaliation.

She had refused to assign him evening classes even though he had taught at least one night class each semester for the previous decade. She had directed office staff members to quietly keep a record of his comings and goings—whether he showed up for classes, whether he was on time, whether he kept his posted office hours, and so on. She had met privately with a number of his students and questioned them extensively about his habits.

She had even issued the unusual request that he turn in his syllabi for the classes he was teaching that semester—an established departmental requirement that had seldom, if ever, been enforced.

"This is sheer harassment," he insisted. "I have always taught night classes." He complained bitterly that the chairwoman's "intrusive surveillance" of his movements constituted "a gross violation" of his privacy: "I have never in my 25 years in the academy suffered such an egregious infringement of my rights."

The professor concluded that the chairwoman "had it out" for him because he had opposed her appointment as department head. The suddenness of her interest in him and the aggressiveness of her surveillance seemed to suggest that she was motivated by a vendetta. He claimed that she had created a hostile workplace, and he demanded that the dean remove her from office. He threatened to involve his lawyer if nothing was done.

The dean was sympathetic. She was a champion of workplace collegiality and had worked hard to ensure that the college maintained its reputation for tolerance and diversity. People on the campus respected her for her keen sense of justice and fair play.

The dean summoned the chairwoman, certain that she had committed serious violations. While waiting for the meeting to begin, the dean contemplated what punishment would be most appropriate. She was determined to send a strong message that the college would not tolerate harassment or retaliation of any type.

Yet when the chairwoman arrived and began to discuss the case, it became clear that the case was not quite so cut and dried. The chairwoman explained that she had been responding to a longstanding problem with the professor. He was notorious in the department for neglecting his classroom responsibilities and other duties.

Most recently, the chairwoman had received a considerable number of complaints from both faculty members and students. His colleagues alleged that he often failed to show up for class, and staff members confirmed that he never registered his absences, as university policy required. A colleague who taught at the same time in an adjacent classroom reported that when the professor did hold a class, he typically ended it halfway through the period.

His students complained that he was inaccessible and had so little contact with them that they were not learning anything. Not only did he frequently cancel or truncate classes, but he rarely held office hours. One student referred to him as her "absent teacher." A few students demonstrated that he graded papers by simply assigning a letter grade on the final page without providing any internal comments—a very unusual practice in his discipline. The students were convinced that he had never even read their papers.

In short, the evidence suggested that the professor was drawing his salary in return for very little work. So the department head had collaborated with officials in human resources to devise a plan that included systematically gathering and documenting information on his classroom attendance. Because she was new to the job, the chairwoman had not thought to inform the dean of the ongoing investigation.

While the chair learned a valuable lesson from this incident—always keep your dean in the loop—the dean learned something, too: Never assume that the version of events before you is true or complete, regardless of how convincing it sounds.

It's a daily reality for most academic administrators that people present us with compelling accounts of some issue in dispute and then implore us to take action based on their version of events. And it's all too easy to leap to the conclusion that the most recent narrative is the "truth"—especially if the issue at hand happens to be a hot-button concern of ours, as was the case with the dean who championed workplace collegiality.

The dean was predisposed to be supportive of victims of retaliation and was already on the alert for discrimination. That's admirable, but it caused her to rush to judgment in this case.

To be effective, academic administrators must possess skills common to seasoned judges: the ability to balance stories and perspectives judiciously before arriving at a decision, to sort through the facts and the various parties' potential motives, to detect whether someone's prejudices are obscuring the facts, and to set aside personal preconceptions and biases.

We all are susceptible to a rush to judgment, especially given our considerable daily workload and our desire to dispose of cases expeditiously. The most effective administrators monitor themselves constantly to avoid potentially costly blunders.

After extensive investigation, the dean ultimately ruled that both narratives contained some truth. The professor was correct that the chairwoman had been quick to initiate her investigation, in part, because she resented his lack of support for her appointment. But the chairwoman was correct, nonetheless, in opening the investigation because the professor was guilty of chronic dereliction of duty and violation of numerous university rules and regulations.

The chairwoman was reprimanded and required to apologize formally to the professor. The professor was given the option to pay restitution to the university, in the form of returning a portion of his salary, or to take early retirement. He chose the latter.

In many ways, such "he-said, she-said" scenarios constitute a kind of administrative gestalt. The key is to be able to look once and see a goblet, look a second time and see two faces, and look a third time and see both images.

Why Rules Matter

Last month's column was about people who attempt to block change by citing rules or interpreting them in the most narrow way possible. But academe also has its fair share of people at the other end of the spectrum: those who ignore rules and deadlines; view them as petty, bureaucratic nonsense; and think they only apply to someone else.

Over the years, I have known several faculty members who refused to submit an annual report summarizing their achievements for the year to their department head. They couldn't be bothered with such trivia, even though failing to do so adversely affected their annual evaluations. Other colleagues would consistently disregard deadlines and submit their grades, sabbatical reports, or other important documents well beyond the published "drop dead" date. Still others, when serving on a committee, would make decisions in direct opposition to the committee's specified criteria—voting to admit to a graduate program someone who clearly did not meet the minimum requirements, for example, or voting against a colleague for tenure even though that colleague had far exceeded the department's stated standards.

Administrators are just as prone to such looseness. I know a social-sciences dean who, in attempting to be compassionate, found himself in hot water with his provost. By university policy, tenure and promotion applications were due by 5 p.m. on a certain Friday. A political scientist called the dean a half-hour before the deadline and frantically begged to hand in his application first thing Monday morning—after all, no one was likely to review the applications that weekend.

The dean generously, but unthinkingly, granted the request, and the assistant professor submitted his application on Monday morning. A week later, a historian in the same college attempted to submit her own tenure application, now a week late. She was told that she was ineligible because she had failed to meet the published deadline. Outraged, she sued the university.

"My provost was furious," the dean told me. "He said I was so intent on playing Mr. Nice Guy that I forgot my duty—to ensure that all faculty and staff in the college were treated with the same degree of fairness." Fearing that the historian would easily win her suit, the university settled the case out of court.

It is not that compassion and flexibility are bad; it is that in violating rules and deadlines, other people might be injured or disadvantaged. A veteran provost I know is fond of saying that a good administrator must be a rule monger, otherwise you invite chaos and injustice. She tells stories of faculty senates or administrative officers creating a rule, and then promptly violating it when that proved convenient. "I would constantly have to remind them that they themselves created the rule, and usually for a good purpose, but they couldn't simply disregard it," she told me. "It is as if some people believe that 'academic freedom' somehow means that they are free from the constraints of rules and deadlines or that rules are for others, not them."

As a kind of master example of why rules matter, consider the set of rules often called a departmental "governance document," or bylaws. As an administrator, I have had to ask people to develop governance documents that clearly articulated in writing the important procedures, rules, and deadlines governing their departments. Doing so has substantial advantages for faculty members, staff employees, and administrators.

The administrative benefits of a well-conceived governance document include:

- **Consistency**. All department members have a reasonable expectation that like situations will be treated in a similar fashion, and fewer decisions are likely to be made ad hoc or on the fly.

- **Accountability**. When procedures, rules, and deadlines are clearly expressed in a publicly accessible document, it becomes much easier to judge proposed actions and behaviors than when no such document exists.

- **Legal protection**. When you make decisions or take actions consistent with your department's formally adopted set of rules and procedures, courts are less likely to decide you have acted in a capricious or discriminatory fashion.

But the rules and policies spelled out in a sound governance document aren't just important administratively. They also benefit faculty members in several ways:

- **Transparency**. The operation of the department is open and comprehensible to all constituents, rather than mysterious and inexplicable.

- **Fairness**. The same consistency that serves as an administrative benefit leads to a greater level of equitable treatment of all department members.

- **Equity**. Rules protect people from the abuses of old-style cronyism. Decisions aren't made capriciously, in smoke-filled rooms, and to the benefit of one person or group over another.

- **Trust**. When decisions are made in the sunshine, when procedures and rules are clearly articulated, and when you are treated in the same fashion as your colleagues, you are much more likely to assume your chair and others are acting in good faith rather than deceptively.

Naturally, when people are able to participate in creating and revising their department's rules, especially the creation of a comprehensive governance document, they are much more likely to buy into those rules and understand why they were adopted and why they are important.

So the key to dealing with people who ignore rules and deadlines is to demonstrate that, while petty bureaucracies do exist, and while some academics do perpetually use rules in obstructive rather than productive ways, rules and deadlines can provide important safeguards against abuse. We need them not primarily as a way to police people but as a way to protect them from unfair treatment.

Rules are like any number of instruments: In the wrong hands, they can become weapons; in the right hands, they are the essential tools we need to get things done.

❖　❖　❖

We Can't Do That Here

Last month, the veteran astronaut Andrew Thomas and several of his colleagues at the Johnson Space Center in Houston posted a homemade video on YouTube. It depicted a fictitious engineer's futile attempts to persuade NASA officials to consider an innovative spacecraft design. At every turn, her ideas were dismissed with statements like "that's not how we operate." Thomas made the video to show how the culture of NASA had become increasingly hostile to new ideas, preferring instead the comfort zone of "the way things are done around here."

In academe—as, apparently, at NASA—people often respond to any proposed change in policy or procedure by saying "University rules prohibit that," or "State law does not allow that," or "Federal regulations specify that we can't do that." Occasionally, no such rule or regulation even exists; it is a figment of lore, faulty memory, or wishful thinking. At other times, the rule may exist but is interpreted so narrowly as to subvert its original intent. Either way, the result is the same: Innovation is trumped by bureaucracy.

A senior sociologist I know ran into such obstacles recently while negotiating an appointment at a lower-ranked institution than his own in order to move closer to his ailing parents. He asked his new department chair for an annual stipend of $5,000 to help defray his research costs, but his request was met with puzzlement.

"The chair claimed that the institution had never given anyone a research stipend and was certain that university rules prohibited it," the sociologist told me. "This university only recently began to raise its research profile, so I think they were just unfamiliar with stipends." Rather than investigate whether there was a way to grant the request, the department head simply took shelter in a comfortable stock reply: "We can't do that here."

A dean of a pharmacy school told me a similar story. He once attempted to install a display case in the hallway outside his office where he planned to exhibit awards and trophies won by his faculty. His plan came to a halt when a campus facilities officer notified him that the case could not be installed because it jutted 10 inches out from the wall and, thus, did not comply with safety regulations.

"I was quite familiar with the regulations," he told me. "And I knew that we were in compliance because the case did not impede access." He challenged the compliance officer to produce the rule. She was unable to do so, and he eventually had his display case installed. But it was a lot of time and effort expended, just to get a display case hung.

An education dean told me of a dispute in one of her departments that serves as yet another example. The department's constitution said that "all tenured and tenure-track faculty shall have the opportunity to evaluate the department chair." Some faculty members read that statement as barring all adjuncts and instructors from weighing in. Others disagreed, arguing that the statement specified no such prohibition.

Asked to make a ruling, the dean pointed out that the statement was simply intended to give faculty members "the right" to evaluate the chair— not to exclude other constituents from the same opportunity. One group in the department had insisted on reading the rule in the most narrow fashion.

Clearly, some perpetually suspicious professors and administrators help foster a culture comfortable with the status quo. Others, in contrast, approach innovation with a can-do attitude: "Let's see if we can make this happen, given our rules and procedures."

Perhaps what I am contrasting are two personality types—one that thinks rules exist in order to police people, and one that sees rules as setting appropriate boundaries. The impulse to ensure that university officials are complying with all relevant rules is a good one; however, rules should not be invoked to cripple a unit or prevent it from forward thinking. And, of course, some people are purely obstructive. They say no for the sheer pleasure of flexing their administrative muscle.

A mix of facts and strategies might help counter those who ritualistically block change.

First, understanding the differences between a rule, a policy, a procedure, and a guideline might be especially helpful. A guideline is simply a suggested practice established to assist people in performing some function, as in "Guidelines for Preparing a Teaching Portfolio." A procedure is a standard practice that a department adopts in order to ensure consistency and efficiency, as in the steps for filing a complaint. A policy is a formally adopted procedure, or set of procedures, that binds people to certain actions, as in a university's alcohol policy. And a rule is an even stronger restriction or prescribed action set by the institution's trustees or some other legal entity, and thus has legal status. Violation of a university rule or policy usually exposes you to serious consequences.

Knowing whether your proposed change would be governed by a university rule or a policy, or if it is merely a matter of procedure, is important. When someone claims the change is "prohibited," you might begin by consulting your institution's formal lists of rules, policies, and procedures to confirm that that is true.

If the rule or policy does exist, the next step is to ask, "Does the rule, in fact, prohibit my proposal, or is someone interpreting the language in an overly narrow way?" Just as there is a huge difference between a guideline and a rule, there is an equally vast gap between "no university employee shall . . ." and "university employees are advised to exercise caution when. . . ."

If you cannot locate the rule, ask someone to show it to you so you can see the precise wording. If people are simply invoking a prohibition as an excuse for saying "we can't do that around here," they will be unable to present the formal, recorded restriction to you.

And, of course, it is always good practice to consult widely on the campus when you propose a change. Having "buy in" from the affected parties helps strengthen your hand against those who tend to block innovation.

It's part of the job for university administrators to comply with all appropriate rules and regulations. But it's also part of the job to seek out new ideas and innovative ways of doing things. If we are to lead our institutions, we need to fight the urge to respond to change with knee-jerk resistance—after all, it's not rocket science.

❖　❖　❖

The Delicate Art of Rejection

A colleague at a nearby university complained to me recently about her department chairman.

"I'm a full professor and a recognized scholar in my discipline, but my chair constantly blocks me from teaching key courses I ask to teach," she said. "To make matters worse, he can never clearly explain the reason for his decision. He usually stares at his shoes and mumbles." She went on to say that lately the chairman had simply instructed his secretary to call her when there is bad news.

A friend of mine who was a finalist for a deanship in a business school expressed a similar complaint. He had survived a grueling three-day campus visit, where it felt like he met half of the people on the campus and most of the local community's senior leaders. He had spent considerable time with the provost, including at a dinner and two private meetings.

"The provost and I hit it off immediately," he said, "and I felt we would have worked well together."

What distressed him even more than not getting the position was the way he was informed of the news. "I received a one-sentence e-mail from the provost's assistant," he moaned. "Was it too much to expect a telephone call after all the time I'd spent with her?"

A paradox of academic administration is that while a key role of department chairs, deans, and presidents is to support and encourage faculty and staff members, our daily experience often involves denying their requests. Qualified applicants for positions, awards, and grants have to be informed that they were unsuccessful this time around. Worthy programs and proposals have to be rejected for one reason or another. And perfectly reasonable requests have to be denied.

No institution—whatever the size of its endowment—has sufficient resources to say yes to every worthy request. Consequently, we find ourselves in the unfortunate position of having to say "no" to our constituents—a lot.

Most of us maintain a precarious balancing act: supporting as many faculty requests as possible, while gently letting down those whose requests must be denied. No wonder a common derogatory epithet for an administrator is "Dr. Jekyll and Mr. Hyde"—too often it can appear that we are professing support on the one hand while withholding it on the other.

No one likes to be rejected, particularly when it concerns a career or pet project. And, in turn, many people feel extremely uncomfortable delivering bad news, especially in person, and so they attempt to avoid unpleasant situations at all costs. When they do finally deliver negative news, their discomfort may cause them to bungle it badly. Feelings are hurt, feathers ruffled, egos bruised.

Because administrators are so often torn between their desire to support people and the fiscal or institutional realities that dictate the denial of many requests, the ability to communicate negative information without alienating the audience has become an essential skill of an effective administrator.

Put simply, "leadership" often means being able to say "no" while continuing to encourage the very person you are rejecting.

I know one university chancellor who has a special talent for conveying negative information effectively. Regardless of the seriousness of the message, he puts his audience at ease, minimizes the listener's discomfort, and cultivates an understanding of why the decision was made. His style of delivery is what makes him so effective: He smiles warmly, looks his audience directly in the eye, and without hesitation or defensiveness demonstrates a genuine understanding of the listener's position and feelings; he then explains the negative news and why it has to be that way.

In short, he is straightforward but supportive. He might begin the session, "Jim, you're not going to like what I have to say. I know you were hoping for increased funding for your center, and I did exhaust all the usual sources, but it just isn't going to happen this year. I'm sure you'll understand that we won't be able to increase funding for ongoing projects until we can cover last year's shortfall, but I promise to make every effort to find you additional funding as soon as I am able." He then would go on at length about the importance of the faculty member's center, that it is indeed a priority, and that there is genuine hope for increased money in the future.

Even if the chancellor could not, in good faith, support a proposal, he would explain—calmly and clearly—why the request is not a priority of the university despite its merits. Petitioners might leave such sessions disappointed, but they always feel that they had been treated fairly and with respect.

That administrator's practice contains all the ingredients of the delicate art of rejection: Look directly at the audience (averting your eyes suggests that you feel guilty about something or that you fear conflict), be transparent and clear, demonstrate that your decision was reasoned and not arbitrary, provide a full explanation of the decision and its context, avoid being defensive or authoritarian, and, above all, treat the listener with dignity and respect.

Perhaps people respond so well to being rejected by that chancellor because he is so direct.

What irritated my friend, the candidate for a business-school deanship, was that the very person he had hoped to work for and with whom he had begun a relationship, now refused to engage him on a personal level. Deans can get very busy, but not that busy!

Failing to engage a finalist directly and personally is a form of cowardice; it is taking the easy way out of a potentially awkward situation. It is avoiding momentary discomfort at the expense of a long-term relationship.

If it is impossible to meet in person with the individual you are rejecting, a telephone call is the next best thing. Recruiting is a courtship, and if you've spent substantial time with a number of finalists for a high-level position, you've begun relationships with them. Just as it would be rude to jilt a lover via e-mail, voicemail, or an impersonal letter, it would be an insult not to inform the runners-up personally. It is the academic equivalent of a "Dear John" letter.

I would go even further and suggest that the same principle ought to apply to searches for entry-level faculty members. If you have brought three candidates to the campus, why wouldn't you want to maintain good will by calling the two who were not chosen for the position? Sure, a few long-distance calls will cost money, but that is a small price to pay for the good will you will have created. Besides, one day you may again be in the position to hire one of them.

Certainly some administrators do not always have the best interests of their petitioners in mind. We all know individuals whose main preoccupation is simply to be in charge and who enact that desire by refusing requests out of hand. Apparently, they derive feelings of power and superiority from saying "no." And some administrators may deny requests for other less-than-legitimate reasons.

But the best academic leaders will strive to support outstanding work, and that means effecting a balance between discovering avenues of support for petitioners and respectfully letting down those who don't make the cut. Above all, it means mastering the delicate art of rejection.

❖   ❖   ❖

Let's Just Do Our Jobs

In a scene in the recent movie *The Departed*, a special-operations officer interviews a young cop to determine if he is suitable to join an elite unit. The officer doggedly attempts to provoke the initiate into losing his cool in order to test whether the neophyte has the necessary maturity and strength of character.

At a crucial point in the interview, the officer growls, "Do you want to be a cop, or do you want to appear to be a cop?" His point is that some people are attracted merely to the power associated with the role of police officer, not to the hard work and risk that go along with doing the job well.

The same can be said of candidates for positions in academic administration: Some are drawn to the potential power and authority—not to the arduous labor that goes into actually being a department head, a dean, or a president.

For purposes of contrast, think of those administrators attracted to the power of the position as "bureaucrats" and those whose first priority is to use power to move an institution forward as true "academic leaders." The former are easy to spot: They just want to be in charge. They have no real vision or desire to advance a department or an institution; they simply want to have people report to them—they want to be "the boss," "the decider." Consequently, they have little investment in change and are quite comfortable with the status quo.

A faculty member I know summed it up best when she complained about her dean: "In four years as dean, she hasn't done anything to lead us. All she's really interested in is being seen as 'big man on campus.' She likes hobnobbing with visiting dignitaries but not helping us solve our very real problems."

To the extent that bureaucrats are overinvested in the idea of being in charge, they will be uncomfortable with the concept of shared governance and will insist on controlling both the decision-making process and the result. They will avoid opening up decision making to a wide constituency because they will always assume that they know best and that the faculty has a skewed sense of the issues. Their administration is likely to be characterized by Star Chamber secrecy, not openness and transparency.

In contrast, true academic leaders are all about change. They want to lead their departments and colleges to new levels of prominence. They want their programs to be among the best of their kind. They are not content with simply "being" in a position.

Academic leaders understand that it is imperative to involve different groups of people in deliberations over important decisions. Good leaders are not preoccupied with being in charge or being the boss but with leading their program toward a particular goal.

A common trait distinguishing those two administrative types is that genuine leaders tend to surround themselves with the best talent available. They seek out the most capable specialists as staff members and supervisors. Genuine leaders often will appoint someone with substantially more knowledge and experience than they possess.

Bureaucrats, in contrast, often feel threatened by especially capable colleagues, interpreting the presence of such individuals as somehow diminishing their authority or ability to be in charge. I know a business dean who, in the space of three years, replaced all five of his department chairs. I was stunned when he told me, "I want them all to know who's boss. They owe me, and they know it."

Such an unabashed admission is shocking because it reveals that the dean's highest priority is not his college but a selfish preoccupation with gaining and maintaining his power.

Because bureaucrats are not motivated to effect change, their default position is to block or deny most requests from those below them. Their constant refrain is "No, we can't do that." Or "There's not enough money for us to take on that project." Or (my favorite) "We've never done it that way before."

The effect of that default position is to stifle innovation and progress. It is easier to say no and be done with a situation than to engage in the kind of creative problem solving that might lead to a workable solution.

The default position of true leaders, however, is to keep an open mind to new and innovative ideas. Their refrain is likely to be "Well, let's explore how we might make that happen." They encourage people to be imaginative and to experiment with more effective and efficient ways to do business.

The disadvantage to being an academic leader as opposed to a bureaucrat is that you always run the risk of making your constituents unhappy with the changes you hope to bring about. Change is unsettling to many people because it means disrupting comfortable norms. So, if your primary concern is simply to stay in office, to appear to be a leader rather than to actually be one, then avoid change at all costs; don't rock the boat.

Obviously, those two portraits are caricatures. Complex management styles cannot easily be reduced to a neat opposition. Yet placing those two exaggerated types in relief is instructive because it sheds light on some important principles of academic administration. And even though I relied on exaggeration to make my point, the fact is that administrators fitting those descriptions do indeed exist. We have all known and perhaps worked with both.

The point is that when we take on administrative responsibilities we also face choices as to what kind of manager we will become. Will we choose to be someone who simply wishes to be in charge, who is suspicious of open decision making, who feels threatened by capable colleagues, and whose default position is to block most requests?

Or will we choose to be someone who attempts to effect productive change, who involves all stakeholders in important decision making, who seeks out the best talent available, and who keeps an open mind to new ideas?

The scene I mentioned from *The Departed* reminds me of a line from another movie that underscores my point nicely. In *The American President*, the lead character, played by Michael Douglas, has an epiphany: "I was so busy trying to keep my job that I forgot to do my job." How many academic administrators, I wonder, could say the same thing?

❖   ❖   ❖

The Cost of Doing Business

At a reception not long ago, a new assistant professor stopped me on the way to the hors d'oeuvres tray and earnestly entreated me to help solve his most exasperating problem: parking.

"It's not fair," he protested. "The 18,000 employees of State Farm Insurance across town are not required to pay a single cent to park, but underpaid professors like me have to pay $85 a year for the 'privilege' of working here at the university."

With an equal degree of frustration, a department chairwoman complained to me about her university's practice of charging a fee to activate data ports—the receptacles in faculty and staff offices that enable computers to be connected to the Internet. "Every time we hire a new faculty member or reallocate space, the tech people charge me $150 a port," she protested. "And all they have to do is flip a switch somewhere."

Those grievances are representative of a common complaint many professors and administrators express about how universities work—that employees and units are often charged fees for work or services they receive from other campus units. That practice, often called "chargebacks," is much misunderstood because it seems counterintuitive: If you are employed by the university, why should you be charged a fee by another part of the institution?

While practices vary, most universities employ a number of internal "cost recovery" measures, especially at public institutions strapped for money. The rationale is that each unit should bear its own weight. A fee-based system allows a unit to become self-sustaining, to pay its own way rather than to become a drain on the institution.

A port-activation fee is a good example. At most universities, a centralized IT division develops and maintains the technological infrastructure. Technology professionals command relatively high salaries given their specialized skills, so an IT unit is expensive to operate. While the cost of universitywide or buildingwide projects will usually be absorbed centrally, chargebacks are a common method of ensuring that those who benefit from specific services help bear the cost.

If your department would like new data ports installed, workers will have to provide an estimate, schedule the job, perform the necessary tasks, troubleshoot, and ensure that everything works properly. That labor (billed at an hourly rate) is a direct cost, as is the cost of materials and supplies.

At times, an institution will subsidize services that are central to its mission. My arts and sciences college, for example, pays for a technology-support group (separate from the university's) that provides faculty and staff members with desktop support and other services at no cost to the user. But there is still a very real expense: That group costs the college close to $500,000 annually. We could have used those dollars to finance other priorities, but enhancing faculty research and teaching through advanced technology is central to the college's strategic plan, and so investing in the group seemed a wise choice.

In effect, those projects and programs that we can't afford to finance are bearing the cost of that collegewide tech service—a kind of invisible chargeback of sorts.

An advantage of a fee-based system is that it introduces an element of accountability. Imagine a university carpentry shop that employs 10 carpenters but has only enough work to keep five of them busy on most days. If the shop were not required to account for its productivity—that is, if the university simply subsidized it and did not charge units for carpentry work—then it might not be clear to anyone that the unit was operating at half capacity and thereby wasting money. In a state university, such poor stewardship would amount to a violation of the public trust.

Ideally, universities will make strategic decisions about which internal services should carry fees. For example, most universities are concerned about how they are depicted in publications produced by their many departments, and so a common practice is to provide professional assistance in the design and layout of departmental brochures, newsletters, and other official documents. The university benefits by helping to prevent the dissemination of amateurish documents—a price well worth the cost.

But even when such a service is provided to departments "free of charge," the services still carry a cost. The office providing the service will keep a precise tally of time and labor, and those expenses will be borne by some unit somewhere in the institution. There is no such thing as a free lunch—or a free university service.

If your campus is unionized, the cost of services is likely to be substantially higher than on nonunionized campuses, adding to the frustration of those attempting to make changes in their programs. One department chairman spent five years trying to determine how he could afford to paint his department's reception area. The estimated chargeback from the unionized paint shop on his campus was so prohibitive that he eventually gave up.

"They wanted to charge me $5,000 to paint our small outer office," he complained. "I could paint it myself on a Saturday afternoon for the price of two cans of paint if they'd only let me."

The true abuse occurs when the university attempts to charge for services that are most appropriately borne centrally; for example, when a department or college is asked to pay for something that is part of the campus infrastructure. Say the university chooses to upgrade fume hoods in all science labs. That is an infrastructural enhancement and not a specific work request (install a new fume hood in Lab 203) and should therefore be absorbed by the university's facilities department.

It is perhaps easier to understand chargebacks related to a specific work order than it is parking fees, but both operate according to similar principles.

My colleague's question about why employees of a local insurance company don't have to pay a parking fee, while he does, is legitimate. Maintaining and expanding parking lots is an expensive proposition. The cost of new parking facilities at one university has ranged from $13-million to $18-million, and the cost per parking space has averaged about $9,000. A few years ago, Harvard University reportedly spent $34-million on a new underground parking facility accommodating 600 vehicles, which translates to well over $56,000 a space. And even surface lots are costly.

A police chief and director of university parking services explained his mission succinctly: "My job is to make money for the university. Whether it's through parking permits or fines, my people are charged with increasing our 'revenue stream' so that we can provide adequate parking for everyone."

That's why the Office of Parking Services on most campuses is so vigilant about enforcing infractions: Collected fines contribute to the dollars needed for maintaining existing parking facilities (restriping spaces, ensuring adequate lighting, and so on) and for financing new and expanded facilities.

All of those activities carry a cost that someone must pay. State Farm and other corporations simply fold the cost of parking into what they charge their customers, and that is why parking appears to be free. Of course, universities could always follow suit and include the real cost of parking (as well as the cost of other services such as port activation) into the tuition they charge, but such measures would ensure that the cost of a college education would become so prohibitive that we would return to the days when only the affluent could afford it.

The practice of assessing chargebacks is not, as I heard one department head characterize it, "the university's attempt to bleed its departments dry." It is, rather, a way to ensure that every unit carries its own weight and is accountable for its own productivity.

Whether you are a department chair trying to balance your priorities or an assistant professor pondering why your parking decal is not provided free for life, the bottom line is that no labor or service in the university (or anywhere else) is free. Someone must pay. Better that we all contribute in our own way.

The Unkindest Cut of All

Over the last year or so, the various online discussion groups devoted to academic administration have been abuzz with chatter about how to manage state-mandated budget cuts. Deans and provosts asked one another for advice about how to handle wide-ranging—and in many cases, unprecedented—rescissions.

As might be expected, each state-supported institution approached the budget crisis from a different perspective on how to maintain—or at least not impair—its mission. Some institutions announced across-the-board pay cuts. Others instituted mandatory furloughs. Still others dismissed or "nonreappointed" adjuncts and full-time temporary faculty members. A few even cut some tenured and tenure-track positions.

A new dean who had never faced state "givebacks" before desperately asked the online group how to go about determining exactly what to cut. Clearly frustrated, she wrote, "We have so little to begin with, everything we have left is important. I can't see how we can prioritize when we have already been cut to the bone."

Another dean replied with what I found to be singularly unhelpful advice. "Simply pass on to your departments the obligation to cut their areas at whatever percentage your state is requiring," she advised. "This places the real responsibility where it belongs—on the individual units."

I agree that when faced with state budget cuts, individual colleges, departments, and units should participate in determining their priorities and recommending what should be eliminated from their own budgets. However, enforcing the same level of cuts across the board is counterproductive. Requiring your very best and most productive programs to be reduced at the same rate as your least productive areas shows a lack of imagination and an absence of strategic thinking.

A more strategic approach would be to analyze which areas of the university are contributing least to its mission and which are helping to propel it forward. When an institution approaches the process from that perspective, it is even conceivable that some areas might gain funds at the very moment that other areas are being trimmed or eliminated.

As you can sense from the frustration of the neophyte dean asking for advice, any budget-cutting process is a fraught time, not only for those experiencing cuts in their departments, but also for those charged with overseeing the reductions. It is painful to eliminate programs, lay off people, or require furloughs. That's why so many institutions take what seems to be the easy way out by imposing across-the-board cuts, as if spreading the pain evenly would somehow mitigate it.

Perhaps more difficult but potentially more rewarding is to make budget reductions disproportionally. While each institution has its own specific priorities and challenges, some general principles are worth considering. Here are a few:

Protect the revenue generators. One college I know always experienced robust summer-school enrollment, which generated much-needed revenue for the institution, yet it chose to eliminate its summer-school budget in a recent round of cuts. The administration was attempting to avoid making other unpleasant cuts, but by eliminating its summer budget it effectively eliminated a source of revenue.

Protect and even nurture your principal programs. Especially protect those that bring national visibility to your institution or help define its distinctiveness. If you must reduce or eliminate programs, it's better to cut ones that are duplicates of those at other institutions than to cut the very areas that set you apart from the pack.

Protect core faculty members. Cutting everyone's salary may seem egalitarian, but it disadvantages the very people who you hope will help move the university forward after the cuts. At my own university, we chose last year to protect the jobs of core faculty members (including clinical faculty members), and instead to eliminate a number of vacant positions and not renew the contracts of a sizable number of full-time temporary faculty members. That was not an easy decision to make. We understood that some of those "temporary" faculty members had actually been employed for many years and had developed close relationships with many people on the campus. But given the university's mission and position as a doctoral research university, our decision to focus the cuts on temporary employees seemed the most reasonable.

Eliminate nonessential personnel and programs first. Careful analysis is likely to demonstrate that any organization employs a number of people whose role is peripheral to the key functioning of the organization. In tight times, those positions should be terminated first. Close down unproductive centers, institutes, and other ancillary enterprises. Many institutions tend to accumulate a surfeit of such enterprises over time, and it is necessary (and healthy) to ask periodically, "Do we really need this center, or has it lost its usefulness?"

Reduce departmental commitments. Just as institutions tend to accumulate centers and other ancillary enterprises that have long since lost their usefulness, some departments accumulate an overabundance of programs. Reducing underperforming majors and minors, for example, can both save money and free up faculty members to engage in more central activities.

Consider mergers. Some departments and programs might thrive if joined together while also saving the university money by eliminating redundant administrative overhead. It might make sense, for example, to combine several small departments into one unit rather than let them limp along as separate entities. An added advantage might be increased collaboration among faculty members.

Seek to reduce the number of administrators when possible. Administrative posts sometimes proliferate just as unnecessary programs do. This is a key area deserving scrutiny whenever budgets are tight. Do we really need a graduate director in our department? Or an associate chair? Does the dean really need a third associate dean?

Institutions tend to grow in an ad hoc fashion, sometimes spawning new programs, employees, and administrators indiscriminately. But the fact that an institution has grown in a certain way does not mean that it must remain that way.

If the budget-cutting exercise of recent months has any silver lining, it is that an institution can pay focused attention to its priorities and potentially emerge leaner but stronger in the end. The "unkindest cut of all" is the one that slices evenly and indiscriminately across all programs without any attention to priorities.

If Only I Knew Then . . .

A scholar I have known for many years was recently appointed dean at her institution, and she called me with a faint note of panic in her voice. She wanted advice, fast: "I need all the help I can find to get me up to speed on how to be an effective administrator. I've never had any training in this area."

She asked me what lessons I had learned as an administrator that I hadn't known as a faculty member. Here is an expanded version of what I told her:

We don't always speak as one. Many faculty members see campus administrators as an allied and coherent group whose members unite, more often than not, to work in opposition to faculty interests. The reality is that any institution is composed of a number of self-contained (though interrelated) areas, and each leader will be preoccupied with making the most persuasive case on behalf of his or her area. Far from a grand us-versus-them conspiracy, what you will inevitably find in any institution will be administrators advocating tenaciously for their particular programs—often in direct competition with other programs.

Bureaucrats or academic leaders? For purposes of contrast, think of administrators as falling into one of those two types. Bureaucrats just want to be in charge. They have no real vision or desire to advance a department; they simply want to be "the boss" and have people report to them. Consequently, they have little interest in change and are quite comfortable with the status quo. True academic leaders, however, are dedicated to productive change. They want their programs to be among the best of their kind. They are not content with simply being in charge. All of us in administration make a choice, consciously or not, as to where on this spectrum we will fall.

Bureaucracy shouldn't trump innovation. In academe, people often respond to any proposed change in policy or procedure by saying "university rules prohibit that" or "state law does not allow that" or "federal regulations specify that we can't do that." Too often, no such rule or regulation exists; it is a figment of lore, faulty memory, or wishful thinking. At other times, such a rule may exist but is interpreted so narrowly as to subvert its original intent. While administrators are required to comply with rules and regulations, it is also part of the job to seek out new ideas. If we are to lead our institutions, we need to fight the urge to respond to change with knee-jerk resistance.

However, get used to saying no. A paradox of academic administration is that while a key role of department chairs, deans, and presidents is to support and encourage faculty and staff members, our daily experience often involves denying their requests. Qualified applicants for positions, awards, and grants have to be informed that they were unsuccessful. Worthy programs and proposals have to be rejected for one reason or another. And perfectly reasonable requests have to be denied. Put simply, leadership often means being able to say "no" while continuing to encourage the very person whose request you are rejecting.

Don't rush to judgment. It's a daily reality for most academic administrators to hear from someone with a compelling account of a dispute who wants us to take action based on that individual's version of events. It is all too easy to leap to the conclusion that the most recent narrative you've heard is "the truth." We all are susceptible to a rush to judgment. The wise administrator waits to hear the competing story, which, inevitably, will be equally compelling. The most effective administrators monitor themselves constantly to avoid potentially costly blunders in rushing to judgment before hearing all sides.

Follow protocol. Proper protocol—the time-honored, orderly, and collegial way of dealing with issues in academe—seems to be deteriorating. Leaping over several layers of authority to take your concerns directly to the president because you believe that will produce the results you want is a breach of protocol. And it's usually counterproductive, since the appeal typically gets kicked back to the appropriate level anyway. We should return to academe's system of professional etiquette. This is an appeal to act responsibly. Avoid falling prey to the immediacy of e-mail, to instant gratification, to the temptation to damage someone's reputation, or to any of the other motives that cause us to violate academic propriety. As in society in general, good etiquette promotes good will; its absence fosters resentment and discontent.

Conduct business as openly as you can. Academic administrators have a responsibility to act in as transparent a manner as possible. Don't just avoid secrecy; promote a climate of openness.

Provide clear explanations of how and why decisions are made, and make budgets and other key documents and procedures available whenever possible.

Understand the philosophy of "chargebacks." A common complaint at most institutions is that offices are often charged fees for work or services they receive from other campus offices. That practice, often called "chargebacks," is much misunderstood because it seems counterintuitive: If you are employed by the university, why should you be charged a fee by another part of the institution? While practices vary, most universities employ a number of internal "cost-recovery" measures, especially at public institutions strapped for money. The rationale is that each unit should bear its own weight. A fee-based system allows each unit to become self-sustaining, to pay its own way rather than to become a drain on the institution as a whole.

Recognize people's accomplishments. Academe now is characterized by an economy of scarcity, and in such an environment, the true cultural capital is proper recognition of good work. Yet too many institutions do a poor job of that. Creating a culture of recognition goes a long way toward improving attitudes and working conditions in any college or university.

Your university computer is not really yours. Many college personnel see campus computers and e-mail accounts as their own private property—a type of employment benefit provided with no constraints on use. In fact, universities "assign" computer equipment and accounts as tools to help us perform our jobs, in the same way that institutions assign offices, laboratory space, or photocopy machines. Computer equipment, far from being personal property, is owned and maintained by the university, with restrictions on how it may be used. That means that use of university computers or e-mail accounts for anything other than university business is a breach of ethics and typically a violation of university policy.

Make friends with fund raisers. University fund raisers are sometimes dismissed or even disparaged by many faculty members as academe's equivalent of used-car salesmen. Fund raising, however, has become an essential tool for fostering the very academic endeavors that we all cherish. Especially given today's economy, it is essential that institutions discover ways to reduce their reliance on state assistance and to attract private dollars. A fund raiser should become your new best friend and ally, not someone to avoid.

"Searching" and "recruiting" are not always the same thing. Building a first-rate academic unit is like developing a successful athletics program. The search process is our opportunity to assemble the ideal team. That means recognizing that passive searching for faculty members isn't enough; to be truly successful, we must actively recruit academics.

Those are some of the key lessons that I mentioned to my colleague who is becoming a dean, but they are central to understanding administrative values and work in general. I only wish that I had understood those aspects of academic administration early in my career as a young faculty member.

As faculty members, we are preoccupied with our own disciplinary concerns and know little about how our institutions actually work. If we were to make the effort to pay attention to other areas of the university, however, we could potentially make our own jobs and working conditions much more tolerable—and even more rewarding. And we would be better prepared for administrative roles.

3

Campus Reform

♦

Carnegie Matters

In January of 2011, the Carnegie Foundation for the Advancement of Teaching announced the results of its most recent classification of colleges and universities. Its previous round of assessment occurred in 2005.

Faculty members and administrations across higher education had eagerly awaited the announcement. A friend of mine who serves as a president of a public university in the South told me that he had spent the last three years leading an effort to position his institution to advance to the next level in Carnegie's designations.

"Our faculty and administration worked in a meticulous way to bring us to that next level," he told me, "and we were all quite gratified when we received notification from the Carnegie people that we had been successful."

Another president was not so successful. She told me that she had attempted to increase various factors on which institutions are judged (the number of doctoral programs, number of doctorates granted, number of postdocs, and so on) to levels that would raise the institution in the "basic classification" designations, but had fallen short.

"We need to become a bit more sophisticated and mature as an institution," she said, "before we will advance to that next rank."

While the Carnegie classifications seem to be watched by most everyone in higher education, there is some confusion about the system and its significance. The foundation classifies the 4,633 institutions of higher education from the smallest, associate-level colleges to the most complex research universities. In doing so, it establishes a valuable continuum on which an institution can assess its complexity and academic diversity.

The confusion derives from conflating the Carnegie continuum with the various "best college" ranking systems, such as the ubiquitous *U.S. News & World Reports* rankings.

The Carnegie foundation's Web site points out that the classification system was developed for the purpose of describing institutional diversity and is, therefore, not a ranking system. It describes an institution according to its undergraduate and graduate instructional programs, its enrollment and undergraduate profiles, its size and setting, and—the category that receives so much attention—its basic classification.

By focusing on describing and classifying institutions, the Carnegie classifications avoid the thankless and impossible task of attempting to judge which institution is superior to another. It is a descriptive, not an evaluative system. In contrast, most of the "best college" rankings set out to do just that: They produce rankings that claim—either explicitly or tacitly—to make qualitative distinctions among institutions.

What makes the Carnegie system particularly valuable is that it relies entirely on official data from federal agencies, primarily the National Center for Education Statistics and the National Science Foundation. It does not solicit data directly from the institutions or conduct opinion surveys. Consequently, its results are especially reliable.

In contrast, for example, *U.S. News* relies on surveys and data directly from the institutions. The *Princeton Review* draws heavily on an extensive survey of student opinions. For its college rankings, *Newsweek* considers student surveys and a range of data available in the popular media, among other factors. *Forbes* even factors in (for a full 25 percent of its formula) student evaluations of professors as posted on Ratemyprofessors.com.

Clearly, those are significantly different types of methodologies from the independent, data-driven formula of the Carnegie classifications. Of course, the "best college" rankings are aimed at prospective students and their parents, while the Carnegie classifications are meant to provide faculty members and administrators with an analytical tool that helps them make valid comparisons and enhance their strategic planning.

That said, institutions have traditionally used the Carnegie system in a host of ways not envisioned by the foundation. Some even use it as a kind of ranking. The two presidents who were attempting to lead their institutions to the next level on the Carnegie continuum were using the classification system as a measure of their progress toward becoming more mature and complex institutions.

In fact, a number of institutions establish in their strategic plans the goal of rising in the Carnegie classifications. That is often a worthy goal because it helps an institution focus on increasing its diversity and complexity.

And traveling up the continuum can have many positive consequences for an institution. In the 1980s I was on the faculty of an institution that rose—quite deliberately, I might add—from Research II to Research I status, categories in Carnegie's original classification system. The prestige that the new designation brought to the university was apparent to all, and a source of great pride among the faculty.

Higher Carnegie status tends to open doors for an institution, perhaps because the confidence level in the institution is higher. Thanks to that higher level of confidence, an institution will very likely enjoy an enhanced ability to attract external grants for research. An institution would most likely be more attractive as a partner to industry, as well. The higher status may also increase an institution's ability to negotiate a higher indirect cost rate for grants from the federal government.

Higher status not only improves an institution's ability to recruit high-quality faculty members, postdocs, and graduate students, it also strengthens the justification for increasing the salaries of faculty and staff members when funding becomes available. That's because faculty salary comparisons, such as Oklahoma State University's well-regarded "Faculty Salary Survey by Discipline," often use the Carnegie classifications as a way of sorting salary levels.

An institution's Carnegie status can also enhance its graduates' attractiveness to prospective employers and to prestigious graduate and professional schools. The Carnegie classifications have become so associated with institutional prestige that they are the cause of competition and even envy between some institutions, as traditional rivals jockey for higher placement.

I know of one perennial state rivalry in which two institutions engaged in a healthy competition with one another in practically every aspect of collegiate life, including athletics, academics, and the arts. One of the two institutions is one level above the other in the Carnegie continuum—a source of great pride for one president and of frustration for the other. The two presidents recently made a friendly wager on whether the lower-ranked institution would rise during the recent reassessment.

I won't reveal who won the bet, but the fact that competition, envy, and friendly wagers are often associated with an institution's Carnegie classification is but one indication that it has become and continues to be a key way that we measure our institutional progress.

Growing Pains

I have joined a number of universities over the years just as they were beginning to ramp up their research profiles. Inevitably, when a university decides to expand its mission, many faculty and staff members experience a certain amount of anxiety. Productivity expectations rise, annual evaluations become more rigorous, tenure and promotion requirements are more demanding, and the institution stops measuring itself against "peer" universities and begins judging itself in comparison with "aspirational" institutions.

Here is a typical scenario: Your university might have begun as a teaching institution. While scholarship was not discouraged, it was not promoted much, either. Faculty members might have been hired, evaluated, and promoted explicitly for their teaching. Some might even have been advised not to worry about producing creative or scholarly work. For as long as anyone can remember, the institution's promotional literature had touted its reputation as one of the finest teaching colleges in the region.

Over time, the institution develops in size and sophistication. Pockets of the faculty begin to produce substantive research and, consequently, forge a reputation for themselves and their university. Imperceptibly, the institution's mission begins to expand, and it starts to see itself as committed both to high-quality instruction and to research. (Critics refer to that phenomenon as "mission creep.")

Eventually, the institution boasts a critical mass of active researchers and reaches a point at which it self-consciously commits to its new mission and goals.

Some faculty members find the transition difficult, and even painful. They feel, and rightly so, that the rules have changed in the middle of the game. They might have been hired decades ago under one set of expectations, and now a whole new set of expectations is in play. Some professors become dispirited, or even bitter, and consider retiring. Others adjust to the changes—some begrudgingly, others enthusiastically.

What you often find at that crucial moment in an institution's evolution is that a minority of faculty members, who have not adjusted well to the change, will remain disheartened and negative. But elsewhere throughout the institution is an almost palpable energy and sense of excitement. Many people on the campus seem to acquire a renewed sense of purpose. Many recommit to their first intellectual love—their disciplines. There seems to be, perhaps for the first time in decades, a sense of common purpose permeating the campus.

As more and more faculty members win grants, publish their papers in top-tier journals, and attract national awards for their work, the institution seems suddenly to experience a renewed sense of self-respect. And more faculty members, staff employees, and students feel a newfound pride in the university.

Not every institution goes through this process or experiences it in quite the same manner, but the pattern is familiar enough for us to draw some useful generalizations.

At first, some faculty members will interpret any change in the mission as a renunciation of the university's past, or a disavowal of those who came before. But that reaction is unwarranted. Universities evolve over time and quite naturally undergo periods of rapid change, punctuated by slower growth or even stasis. In fact, the reason the university has arrived at a stage at which it is poised to move forward is the hard work of those faculty members and administrators who prepared the way.

Perhaps inevitably, some professors will complain that the university no longer values good teaching or that increased attention to research will degrade the quality of education students receive. Nothing can be further from the truth. Teaching and research have a symbiotic relationship. Students learn best when they work alongside professors on their latest research projects and gain firsthand knowledge of how scholars work.

Despite the typical complaints that researchers are only interested in their careers and not in students, I will go so far as to say that the very best teachers—at any level, but especially at the graduate and upper undergraduate levels—are those who remain active in their fields and are most familiar with the cutting-edge knowledge of their disciplines.

Another anxiety that some faculty members experience is their belief that increased research means only externally financed research—projects supported by grants that bring dollars into the university. Certainly, grants not only support specific projects but also contribute to the larger research enterprise. The more external grants brought in, the more resources a university has to fuel its many projects and programs. In addition, successful researchers are able to pay for part or all of their salaries from their grants, further freeing up money for other institutional priorities.

But "research" is a broad term and refers to much more than externally financed projects. Clearly, not every discipline can attract the same level of grant support. Historically, there is substantially less money available to the humanities than to other disciplines (although that fact has caused too many humanists to fail to apply for the grant money that does exist, thereby ensuring that they never receive a dime).

Faculty in disciplines with limited grant opportunities often become very nervous when they hear that their university plans to give high priority to research, because they erroneously assume that that refers only to external grant projects.

The real point behind most drives to ratchet up research is not simply to generate additional dollars but to achieve ever-greater levels of national prominence. Garnering high levels of external funding is one way to increase prominence, but there are many others, and they are all tied to the specific kinds of intellectual work we do.

If you were to imagine a utopian university, all of your faculty members would be leaders in their fields. Many would be Guggenheim fellows, Rhodes scholars, MacArthur fellows, and inductees into the National Academies. Your humanists would be Pulitzer and Nobel Prize winners; your mathematicians would be Fields Medal recipients; your actuarial students would be Wooddy scholarship winners; your music professors would regularly debut new compositions at such venues as Carnegie Hall. Such achievements come true when your creative and scholarly work has become so influential that it catapults you (and your institution) to prominence.

A university's reputation skyrockets as a result of individual accomplishments, and that, in turn, engenders increased confidence in the university on the part of donors and grants agencies, causing them to invest even more in what they perceive to be a winning enterprise, and on and on.

In short, the message an institution is sending when it sets out to raise its research profile is simply for you as a faculty member to do what you can do best: Engage actively in your discipline. Become a player in your field. That's not the "careerist" (i.e., selfish) act that some portray it to be, because the greater your success, the more your students and institution will benefit. Your success contributes directly to your institution's success, and vice versa.

Like actual growing pains, institutional growing pains are not easy. You may experience awkwardness and discomfort in the short term, but the end result is well worth it: greater institutional maturity and a general feeling of satisfaction about being part of an institution with higher standards and aspirations, and increased respect nationwide.

❖ ❖ ❖

Why Universities Specialize

In a surprise action taken in February of 2012, the Idaho State Board of Education—the policy-making body for all public education in the state—stripped the University of Idaho of its flagship status. The Board also declared that Idaho State University could no longer claim "statewide leadership" in the health professions, and that Boise State University must refrain from stating that it "provides leadership in academics, research, and civic engagement."

The stated rationale for these actions was that the Board was reluctant to elevate one state university over another because doing so might encourage them to compete with one another rather than work together collaboratively. Words such as "flagship" and "leadership" seemed to signal one institution's superiority over the others.

In an equally surprising action, the University of Idaho defied its own governing board by posting on the main page of its website a detailed argument as to why it is in fact the state's flagship institution of higher education after all. It asserted that by stripping the institution of flagship status, the Board had "refused to recognize the University's role as the state's first university, the state's land-grant university, the state's leading research university, and the state's primary doctoral degree-granting university—all elements of a nationally accepted definition of flagship."

While these actions are of no consequence to anyone outside of the state of Idaho, they do occasion reflection on why the universities within a state typically have distinct missions that set them apart from one another and why traditionally this has been thought of as advantageous for higher education within a state.

Most states designate one university in the state as the flagship. For centuries, the word "flagship" has been used to refer to a naval fleet's lead ship, the vessel bearing the fleet's flag and commander. By analogy, we use the term also to refer to a state's lead university—the institution that sets an example for the other institutions in the state to aspire to.

While the criteria used to determine which institution to confer that honor on will vary from state to state, typically a state's flagship is its land-grant institution. It is likely to be the university with the highest research profile and the most doctoral programs. It may have the state's medical school, law school, or both. And it may be the largest and best endowed university in the state. Membership in the prestigious Association of American Universities may be yet another factor, and NCAA Division I athletics is a must.

These are the types of considerations that typically cause one institution in the state to be known (if not officially designated) as the flagship university. In most instances, there is no dispute as to which university is a state's flagship. Most everyone would recognize the University of Wisconsin at Madison or the University of Michigan at Ann Arbor or the University of Colorado at Boulder as their states' flagships, for example.

So in the case of the state of Idaho, while the State Board has the authority to instruct the University of Idaho not to use the word "flagship" to describe itself, this does not change the fact that it is the state's land-grant institution, that it is the only public institution with a law school, and that it outpaces the other state institutions in research and graduate education. It is, in other words, de facto the state's flagship regardless of any "official" designation.

Of course, in large, complex states it may not always be so easy to identify the flagship. During the 1980s and 1990s when I lived and worked in Florida, no one questioned that the University of Florida was the state's flagship. It is a member of the Association of American Universities; it has both a medical and a law school; it is a land-grant, sea-grant, and space-grant university; and it is typically ranked among the top public universities in the nation.

Today, however, the University of Florida, Florida State University, and the University of South Florida list themselves as the "three co-flagship universities" in the state, which gives rise to the amusing image of a naval fleet with three separate commanders in three separate ships leading the fleet undoubtedly in three separate directions.

Of course, the flagship designation is not the only way that universities distinguish themselves from their sister institutions in a state. More often than not, one university in a given state (perhaps, the University of . . .) will have the law school, another (often, Such and Such State) will have the medical school, while the so-called directional schools (the University of

North This and South That) will have missions focusing on teacher education, or engineering, or other professional areas.

This kind of institutional specialization makes good sense from a number of perspectives. First, it allows institutions within a state to develop their own unique identities. An institution's distinct identity is what helps it develop a reputation for excellence in specific academic areas, which in turn helps drive student (and faculty) recruitment and retention. It is also a major factor in producing a climate of school spirit among students and alumni, which, of course, may pay off in fundraising efforts. Students want to be in a position to brag that they attended the state's finest teacher education college, or the state's premier business college, or the state's flagship.

In addition, specializing makes good business sense, which is especially important in light of the economic crisis that higher education has faced of late. Because specializing minimizes unnecessary duplication (why support two competing law schools in a small or medium size state?), a state is able to manage scarce higher-education dollars more economically. That is, when universities in a state carve out distinct academic identities, the overall system of higher education operates with greater efficiency.

In fact, one of the principal goals of effective strategic planning for any institution of higher education is precisely to establish which areas of excellence and distinction to focus on and further develop, which means deciding which programs to invest resources in. A good strategic plan will serve as a blueprint for an institution to build on its strengths and solidify its reputation for excellence in those academic areas.

A good analogy might be to graduate education. Few universities can be all things to all people when it comes to types of graduate programs, so they specialize. One institution might have a nationally respected doctoral program in psychology, but only a mediocre sociology program. A university in the adjoining state might have one of the top sociology programs in the country but not a well-respected psychology program. The same dynamic is often true of institutions themselves, especially within a state's borders.

Besides, a healthy competition among a state's institutions can have a positive effect, causing them to strive harder to become better than their sister institutions in certain areas—or at least better than they themselves used to be. Without such competition, the University of South Florida and Florida State would not have become the powerhouse research universities that they now are as quickly as they did. Undoubtedly, the legendary state university rivalries—Clemson and the University of South Carolina, say, or Auburn and the University of Alabama—have done much to help those institutions grow as well.

So, while from time to time state boards of education become concerned about competition among its universities, specialization among the colleges within a state's borders is more the rule than the exception, and it can even play a positive role in improving higher education in a state.

Why Universities Reorganize

Last month I received an e-mail advertising an online seminar called "Academic Restructuring: Guidelines for Academic Leaders." The blurb promised to help administrators who are leading reorganization campaigns. How? By detailing proven methods to prevent morale problems, and even attrition, among faculty members disenchanted with the change.

The idea that a proprietary concern would market a seminar on how to manage the damage control from a campus reorganization is but one indication of how ubiquitous such efforts have become in higher education.

The current fiscal crisis has been a major impetus for colleges and universities to undertake reorganizations, but, more often than not, institutions report a combination of reasons:

- In 2009, Arizona State University announced its second major academic reorganization within a six-month period. It involved more than a dozen of its schools, colleges, and institutes. While university officials touted the substantial "intellectual synergies" that would result from the changes, they also hoped to save close to $3-million in the process. University press releases proclaimed that the changes would "not reduce ASU's academic offerings, eliminate any tenured or tenure-track appointments, or diminish access for students."

- At the same time, Northeastern University undertook its third major restructuring in the past dozen years. The administration divided its College of Arts and Sciences into three smaller colleges and redesignated its College of Criminal Justice as a school within the newly formed College of Social Sciences and Humanities. Northeastern's provost told the *Alumni Magazine* that the administration made the changes to aid the university's "transformation to a more academically selective institution with a higher research profile."

- Also in 2009, Florida Atlantic University announced a reorganization that would eliminate 170 faculty and staff positions, 140 of which were already vacant. The 30 layoffs included five tenured professors in the university's College of Engineering and Computer Science. Officials declared that the changes were in response to a nearly $17-million cut in state support.

- In 2010, the University of Northern Iowa reduced its number of administrative divisions from four to three, thereby eliminating a vice president's position, and it trimmed its number of colleges by merging its College of Natural Sciences and the College of Humanities and Fine Arts. The university's provost was quoted as saying that the restructuring was intended to strengthen academic offerings as well as trim administrative costs to best serve the needs of students.

- Similarly, Eastern Washington University's response to recent budget cuts was to reorganize its academic units, including reducing the number of colleges from six to four and reconfiguring several academic departments.

At my own campus, Idaho State University, we undertook an extensive process to devise a reorganization plan. Four faculty committees held 57 meetings, eight of them public forums, to investigate proposed changes. We began with three primary goals: to reorganize units in such a way as to increase efficiency and streamline operations; to enable our institution to emerge from a period of fiscal challenge academically stronger, not weaker; and, if possible, to realize a financial savings that could be applied to the state's substantial and continuing budget cuts for higher education.

We accomplished all three of those goals with a reorganization plan that was eventually approved by the State Board of Education. Briefly, we consolidated the College of Pharmacy and the College of Health Professions to create the Division of Health Sciences. We merged science departments from the College of Arts and Sciences with the College of Engineering to create a College of Science and Engineering. And the remaining departments in the College of Arts and Sciences became the new College of Arts and Letters.

One of our main goals, besides creating more academically viable units, was to emerge from stringent state budget cuts without having to lay off faculty and staff members, mandate furloughs, or make across-the-board salary cuts. We managed to accomplish those objectives, in large part because of the savings realized from the reorganization.

Clearly, the two dominant themes in our reorganization, and countless others over the last few years, have been realizing savings that could be applied to a substantial budget cut and creating more efficient and academically sound units.

A reorganization usually doesn't just affect academic departments. Part of the major changes at Northern Iowa involved eliminating the division of marketing and advancement. At Idaho State, not only did we reorganize academic units, but we downsized areas in student affairs and consolidated academic student-support units under a single umbrella, the newly formed Student Success Center, which should allow us to improve student retention. Other universities have reorganized units within finance, administration, and athletics.

The reorganization trend in academe has caused a great deal of apprehension, and even anger, among some faculty members. A colleague who recently attended a two-week training session for new provosts reported to me that fully half of the attendees claimed that their institutions were considering or had already undertaken a reorganization of academic units and, of those institutions, more than three-quarters were facing the threat of no-confidence votes against the provost, the president, or both.

Faculty unrest over restructuring is becoming quite common. When Middle Tennessee State University reorganized its academic units recently, some professors staged protests on the president's lawn. And at Idaho State last spring, the faculty held two votes, first against our reorganization plan and later against me as the chief academic officer—that despite the fact that we had protected every faculty and staff position on the campus.

The obvious question: Why is there so much faculty dissent nationwide about campus reorganization efforts—so much that proprietary organizations are now offering seminars on how to manage the damage control?

One answer is that change is difficult for anyone, but that seems to be especially true for academics whose training and professional lives are guided by decades-old traditions. Many faculty members find it difficult to imagine a way of doing things different from what they are accustomed to, despite the promised benefits of a reorganization.

A fellow provost who had faced considerable opposition to reorganization on her campus said to me, "I don't know why the faculty are so threatened by restructuring. It's like cleaning out and reorganizing your closet at home for a more efficient use of your space. It just makes good sense."

Having experienced major reorganizations on more than one campus in my career, I can report that major change always seems to generate considerable angst. But the corollary to that anxiety is that once the change is in place, many who once opposed it often begin to embrace it. What once seemed so foreign and unimaginable soon becomes a source of optimism as faculty and staff members begin to realize the benefits of the new organization.

Perhaps if, from the outset, more of us avoided a knee-jerk resistance to change and instead attempted to imagine the possibilities, there would be little need for campus unrest, no-confidence votes, or seminars on damage control.

❖ ❖ ❖

The Importance of External Boards

In a recent Internet discussion among academic deans, the topic was whether departments and other academic units should create external advisory boards. The dean who raised the issue asked his colleagues whether they maintained boards, if they were genuinely beneficial, and what the ideal board would look like.

Some administrators are only now recognizing the value of advisory panels, but they have become indispensable to many academic units.

While business schools once enjoyed a virtual monopoly on the practice, today high-level external boards are ubiquitous. (My college operates four, and a number of our departments have, or are establishing, their own.)

Still, as the deans' online discussion showed, a wide range of views exists about the best way to organize such boards and about their relative value.

Presidents, deans, and department heads create external boards with a variety of objectives in mind, but they are most useful as tools to solicit strategic or programmatic advice, cultivate political influence, and support fund raising.

Advisory boards can take a number of forms. Among the most common: the community advisory board, composed of influential political and community leaders; the alumni board, made up of distinguished graduates; the professional board (often a specialized kind of alumni board), devoted to a specific career such as law or medicine; the emeritus faculty board; and the development board, which assists in fund raising.

The benefits of well-managed boards are many, but the key one is that they get people actively involved in the department or the college. Once board members are fully invested in the institution, they are more likely to support it financially and in other material ways.

Consider the experience of one departmental advisory board that included an alumnus who had just ended a long and productive career as president of several universities. He took it upon himself to become the department's champion and leveraged his considerable influence to raise an enormous amount of money for the department. My own college recently raised more than $180,000—largely from members of our external advisory boards—to endow a series of faculty and staff recognition awards.

External boards can benefit almost any academic unit. I know a president of a large but remote state university who has effectively extended his university's reach well beyond its geographical confines by establishing a number of "regional" advisory boards throughout the state. He appointed key political and community leaders as well as local alumni to the boards. Those groups have helped him acquire an unprecedented level of state support for his institution.

That kind of cultivation of friends is essential at this moment in higher education, especially in public institutions, where many universities report that the state provides less than 30 percent of their annual budget. In establishing a board, you might consider a number of best practices:

- One rule of thumb is to assemble a board of between 25 and 30 members, assuming that any given meeting will likely draw approximately half of the participants.

- Balance the original list of invitees carefully (keeping in mind such characteristics as gender, race, region, departmental or collegial affiliation, and so on).

- For best results, invite each potential board member personally—by phone or in person. A direct invitation signals that you take the project seriously and allows you to explain your vision of the board's objectives and the member's role. Your energy and enthusiasm will persuade people to participate. No letter or e-mail invitation would ever be as effective.

- Although advisory boards, by definition, possess no authority over your department or college, treat them with the same attention and deference that you would a governing board. Your evolving relationship with the members will be likely to cultivate a culture of giving among the group.

- Compose (with board input) formal bylaws and procedures to regulate the mission, objectives, election or appointment of members and officers, and so forth.

- Because high-level boards are composed of influential people whose busy schedules will make it difficult to assemble everyone together at any given time, it is advisable to meet only two or three times a year and to schedule the meetings many months in advance.

- Crucial to the success of any panel is the selection of a productive chair, someone with whom you get along and who will guide the group toward your objectives.

- Much like a trustees' meeting, an advisory-board session should be held in a respectable venue (a corporate board room, perhaps). It should be organized according to a formal agenda, and include packets of relevant documents and supporting materials.

- To be effective, a meeting can't simply be a recitation of the college's accomplishments or the department's recent points of pride. People agree to serve on a panel because they want it to be useful, and they are acutely aware of unnecessary drains on their time. Meetings, then, must present genuine issues and provide ample time for discussion.

- Support the board with a dedicated Web site that includes the bylaws, minutes of meetings, photos and short bios of members, and other relevant materials. The site serves a utilitarian function but also showcases the support your department or college has from important people.

- Keep your board members engaged. Some experts advise that you stay in touch with members between meetings by periodically calling them or meeting them individually for lunch to ask their advice on an issue. You've brought them into the circle, so use them.

- Finally, determine whether to require board members to pay dues. Business schools typically levy a substantial annual dues payment. The amount may be as little as $2,000, or as much as $50,000, or more. Of course, in the business milieu, the dues probably would be paid by the member's business or corporation, not by the member personally. You will have to make that decision based on your own context. One dean of a college of education told me, "We chose not to require dues because we felt that doing so might discourage some prospective members from joining."

Of course, external boards can present challenges as well as opportunities. Many administrators establish an advisory panel because they genuinely wish to solicit advice. But board members need to understand from the outset that their "advice" is just that—recommendations that the college may or may not act upon. Stories abound of boards or individual members who have engaged in heavy-handed attempts to dictate direction or priorities.

That was precisely the scenario when the alumni advisory board for a small liberal-arts college locked horns with its president over the general-education curriculum. "My board chair insisted that we adopt a great-books approach to gen-ed," the president told me. "I tried to explain that our faculty governance system has an elaborate procedure for making such changes and that the faculty had twice rejected a great-books orientation." The pressure eventually reached such a level that the president disbanded the board.

To avoid such conflicts, the bylaws should clearly specify that the external board has no policy-making authority and that it exists only to serve as a sounding board for the dean or president. Members need to be advised of that from the beginning of their appointment, and it is wise to exercise control over which items are placed on the agenda.

Another safeguard is to make sure that the bylaws contain term limits for members so that someone can be eased off the board if necessary.

Still, the potential benefits of these boards outweigh the occasional conflicts. A well-managed advisory board can be an effective advancement tool, in the largest sense of the term: It can help you publicize your unit's accomplishments, cultivate potential donors, nurture existing ones, and extend your program's influence and support.

❖ ❖ ❖

Certifying Online Research

A department chairman from a nearby university recently solicited my advice on how to handle a tenure case in which the candidate's entire body of scholarship consisted of online publications.

The candidate was a valued colleague, but the department's faculty members were "extremely conservative" in their definition of acceptable scholarly work, the chairman told me. He worried that he would lose his young colleague to what he termed "generational prejudices."

"Our university has no formal policy governing electronic scholarship," he told me. "And, quite frankly, I'm in no position to judge it myself."

That anxiety was echoed by a dean of education who complained at a recent professional conference that faculty members in her college were "deeply divided" over how to evaluate electronic scholarship. Professors in her college's curriculum and instruction department readily embraced many forms of "e-scholarship," while faculty members in other departments seemed unreceptive or even hostile to those emerging forms.

"What am I supposed to do?" she implored in exasperation. "One group sees itself as avant-garde and riding the wave of the future; the other sees itself as upholding standards against the corrosive force of technophilia. I, as dean, am stuck in the middle."

Those two scenarios illustrate a growing area of concern for tenure committees and academic administrators throughout higher education: Exactly how do we arrive at a judicious assessment of scholarship present-ed in various forms of new media? How do we acknowledge and reward substantive electronic scholarship that genuinely furthers knowledge in a discipline, while avoiding the awarding of undue credit to less worthy work?

The digital revolution has substantially improved scholarly work, but it has also brought challenges to those of us charged with overseeing our institutions' tenure, promotion, and rewards processes. While several elec-tronic forms compete for legitimacy, the two most prominent are journals published exclusively online, and Web sites devoted to scholarly subjects.

As more and more electronic journals adopt peer-review processes that replicate the rigorous ones employed by established print journals, many e-journals are acquiring reputations for comparable rigor. Over time, each discipline will arrive at a general consensus about the status of various e-journals in the same way that they once did for print journals.

Scholarly Web sites, however, present a unique set of challenges to college administrators.

In the print world, scholars generally agree about which sources are reputable. All notable scholarly presses thoroughly vet each project, and certain venues have gained reputations for conducting especially rigorous peer reviews. No such formal gatekeeping, in contrast, is in place for the scholarly sites on the Internet.

A Web site devoted to a celebrated literary critic, for example, purports to contain the most comprehensive bibliography of his oeuvre, but the bibliography is far from comprehensive and is riddled with errors. Simply put, the site is not dependable.

As it turns out, it is operated by a student—which, in and of itself, is not necessarily a problem. But the point is that it is not always possible to ascertain exactly who is operating a site—a senior scholar, an entry-level assistant professor, a graduate student, or even a nonacademic.

And since no vetting mechanism for scholarly sites exists, even those that are designed by reputable scholars typically undergo no formal review. Such uncertainty disrupts the orderly intercourse of scholarly activity and plays havoc with the tenure-and-promotion system.

Clearly, the scholarly community needs to devise a way to introduce dependability into the world of electronic scholarship. We need a process to certify sites so that we all can distinguish between one that contains reliable material and one that may have been slapped together by a dilettante. We need to be able to ascertain if we can rely on a site for our own scholarship and whether we should give credit toward a colleague's tenure and promotion for a given site.

With those goals in mind, I propose the following:

- The major professional and scholarly organizations in each discipline should devise a certification process in which a site owner can apply to have a site reviewed and recognized, perhaps for a nominal processing fee. The site would be subjected to a formal and rigorous review by peers in the disciplinary area covered by the site.

- Only those sites meeting the highest standards should be awarded certification.

- Once a site wins certification from the national scholarly society, it should be permitted to display that stamp of approval prominently.

- The certification should remain in effect for a specific and limited amount of time (since a site can change rapidly and without notice). The site should regularly seek renewal of its certification.

- Each disciplinary organization should issue a resolution recommending that departments construe certification of a site as indicating that it has met the highest standards of scholarship.

- Each organization should maintain an online registry of certified sites.

Only an accreditation process of that sort will resolve the principal obstacle to evaluating research published online. And only our most prestigious learned organizations can be trusted to review and endorse works of scholarship to the satisfaction of all involved. A certification process would give working scholars a modicum of faith in digital resources, and would enable tenure committees and administrators to make informed decisions.

While Internet aficionados might object that traditional print forums are not subjected to a similar certification process, conventional venues do not publish works regardless of their quality. All university presses and most scholarly journals are refereed, and the few journals that are not refereed at least have some gatekeeping in the form of the journal's editor.

Internet sites, in contrast, have no such mechanisms for quality control, and that is precisely why some kind of official recognition is necessary.

Some critics might object that the Internet and the scholars who publish online can regulate themselves, but I am not proposing "regulation." I am calling for a voluntary process of certification. Site owners would be free to seek certification—or not.

"Self-regulation" will not solve the primary problem—namely, that there is simply no way to know whether a site is dependable.

Other people might object that it would be difficult to construct guidelines governing site quality that are applicable from site to site. Yet scholars in each disciplinary area already judge the quality of scholarship every time they referee a manuscript for a university press or print journal. That process has worked well.

In fact, who better to judge the quality of scholarship in a field than peers active in that area? Certainly, each institution will need to articulate precisely how it will value electronic scholarship. But no colleague should be lost over "generational prejudices"—or, for that matter, tenured because a department could not detect substandard scholarship.

It behooves the disciplinary organizations to play an active role in instituting a mechanism of quality control for scholarly Web sites. The alternatives—chaos, or evaluation by nonexperts—are unacceptable.

❖   ❖   ❖

Why Universities Are Streamlining Their Curricula

In my state, the provosts of public colleges and universities meet formally every other month as the Council on Academic Affairs and Programs to discuss education issues of statewide import, such as new degree programs. The sessions are part of the formal governance structure of higher education here, and at least one member of the state board typically attends.

Before a new degree program can be forwarded to the state board for approval, it must be OK'd by the provosts' council. For example, the provosts must be satisfied that the new program does not duplicate a similar one in the state, and that it meets the work force needs of the state and the nation—that is, that graduates would have a reasonable expectation of securing employment with the degree.

At a council meeting a few months ago, we were discussing a new Ph.D. program proposed by one of the state's universities, when a state board member said, with obvious frustration, "You provosts keep asking us to approve new programs, but where are the program closures? How can we as a state afford unchecked expansion of academic programs without a commensurate reduction of unproductive programs from our books?"

It was a valid point. That savvy board member understood that curricular glut—as it is called in academic circles nationwide—is threatening to make our institutions inefficient and sluggish. We have become so overcommitted in course requirements and programs that it is threatening our ability to provide adequate support of our healthy academic programs.

Many colleges and universities are re-examining their curricula and assessing what should be trimmed and what should be enhanced. Generally, institutions are scrutinizing three key areas of reform: general-education requirements, requirements within majors, and underperforming programs.

The dire financial situation for higher education in most states has accelerated the process of streamlining, especially the elimination of weak programs. The University of Maine created an Academic Program Prioritization Working Group to analyze which programs to cut, and in what order, to meet budget reductions while maintaining high-priority academic programs. The group's final report is appropriately titled "Achieving Sustainability."

The State University of New York at Albany recently announced that it would close programs in the classics, French, Italian, Russian, and theater. Student demand for those programs is ebbing nationally, and many institutions are finding they don't have the budget to keep marginal programs afloat.

Faculty and staff members often oppose program closures. In response to the SUNY announcement, the American Association of University Professors recently urged the SUNY president to reconsider. And a national petition is being circulated that expresses "concern and dismay" over the elimination of the language programs (but not, apparently, over closing the classics and theater programs). As of the writing of this column, the petition had 13,691 signatures.

I understand those strong feelings. But there seems to be a pronounced lack of understanding as to why universities find program closures to be a necessary and, in many cases, positive action.

As an example, consider a fictional languages department at a public university. Let's assume that the department's program in Spanish is thriving: Student demand for courses and degrees is unprecedentedly high, and each semester the department must turn away many students.

The faculty members in the Spanish program are stretched thin. Their courses are always full, and sometimes they even teach an extra course or two with no compensation just to help the students clamoring to get into or through the program. Unlike some of their colleagues teaching other languages in the department, the Spanish faculty members are operating well beyond capacity. They are so overextended that they don't have time to serve on collegewide committees, and their research productivity is suffering because they are so focused on serving their students.

In contrast, professors in the Serbian languages program in our fictional department have a much lighter workload. The program's three professors teach a handful of students, and it only graduates one to two a year, the same number as it has annually for more than a decade. Typically, a Serbian course will enroll between two and five students. Meanwhile, in the very next classroom, a Spanish professor will be teaching an overflow course of 40 students.

What's wrong with that picture?

That scenario is fairly representative of a basic inequity that can develop among faculty members within the same department. Certain professors are stretched beyond capacity, teaching and advising record numbers of students, while their colleagues in the same department teach a fraction of that number for the same compensation. Scenarios like that are why colleges nationwide are re-examining their curricula. Departments have a set budget and a mission to provide instruction, but their budgets cannot possibly finance all of the courses and programs that faculty members favor. Something has got to give.

At that point, hard questions need to be asked. At our fictional institution, the questions would be: Can we really support a major in Serbian? Should we close the program and shift the resources to the burgeoning Spanish program? Alternatively, should we discontinue the major in Serbian (so long as the major is in the catalog, the courses must be offered) and instead offer only a minor or a few electives?

Let's say the three instructors in the Serbian program together make $240,000 annually, excluding benefits. And at any given time, there are 20 students in the Serbian program in one capacity or another. Let's also assume that the department typically hires two adjunct faculty members to help cover the required courses in the major. Combined, the two adjuncts cost the department another $60,000 in wages. While the tenured and adjunct instructors may well be teaching other language students, together they are supporting a major that costs their department in excess of $300,000. Ignoring benefits and all the ancillary costs, this department is spending in excess of $15,000 per student to maintain this major—and it is unlikely in most public institutions that a student's tuition would cover those costs.

The question, then, for the chair and faculty of the languages department becomes, "Is it an appropriate expenditure of departmental resources to support the Serbian program at this high cost while Spanish is overwhelmed?"

A member of the Serbian faculty might answer, "No self-respecting university in this day and age would not offer a major in Serbian." But that answer ignores the underlying problem. The program is not supporting itself; it is, in effect, being subsidized by other programs on the campus—Spanish, in particular.

Of course, a private college—especially a well-endowed one—might well make a conscious decision to subsidize an otherwise unsustainable program for one reason or another. Maybe the program is central to the college's mission, or it is the only one of its kind and therefore brings distinction to the campus. But in an age of shrinking state support for higher education, most public universities do not have that luxury.

Public institutions have an obligation to be fiscally responsible, to protect the public trust. Maintaining underperforming and floundering programs at the expense of healthy programs violates that trust. What's more, it is unfair to students, because subsidizing unsustainable programs drains support from the healthy ones.

Substitute the word "German" for the word "Serbian" in this example and now you know a dilemma that many language departments are facing across the nation. Institutions are struggling with whether they should discontinue their German majors for the very reasons I have been discussing. Really, though, the precise discipline is beside the point. The reality is, healthy institutions regularly examine their programs for viability, whether they are in the sciences, the social sciences, the professions, or the humanities.

The same dynamic is at play with other types of curricular streamlining; for example, reforming general-education requirements that are needlessly inflated. Curricular glut makes programs and institutions operate inefficiently and disadvantages both students and faculty members. Students are crippled because unnecessary requirements decrease the students' likelihood to graduate in a timely manner. And faculty members are challenged because the more curricular commitments a department has, the more difficult it is for professors to find time to pursue other objectives, such as research and creative activities.

In short, the curricular reform that is under way throughout higher education is, first and foremost, about serving our students. It's about streamlining general-education requirements so that they can progress in a timely manner. It's about making sure that a major's requirements don't place unnecessary hurdles in students' way. And it's about trimming underproductive programs so that adequate resources can then be invested in programs with strong enrollment.

We owe it to our students—and the public, in general—to operate as efficiently as possible.

❖   ❖   ❖

Should We Ditch Football?

In recent years, some colleges have eliminated their football teams or drastically reduced their athletics programs, in response to fiscal crises. But are sports teams really a drain on academic budgets?

Among the institutions that have announced plans to eliminate their football teams are California State University at Northridge (after 40 years), Hofstra University (after 69 years), Northeastern University (after 74 years), and Western Washington University (after 107 years). Those universities decided that their investment in one or more athletics programs was not paying sufficient dividends.

Often when a university announces plans to close a program, officials will, in the next breath, mention the potential cash savings. I remember reading that Hofstra hoped to save $4.5-million by eliminating its football program, money the university would then reallocate to scholarships and other expenses.

Historically, when budgets get tight, athletics programs have been a favorite target of some faculty members and administrators. That's not the case at institutions with highly successful teams, but for those with mediocre athletics programs, many constituents find it tempting to sacrifice an underproductive team to the greater good of the institution.

An athletic director at a midsize research university told me about his constant struggle over this issue with the faculty senate on his campus. "Every few months or so, one or more senators would attempt to pass a resolution stating that the senate recommends dumping our football team," he said. "It's true that our team has not been competitive for some years, but what is very frustrating is that these senators have no idea of how much even a mediocre team brings to an institution."

He pointed out that, not long before our conversation, a donor had made a substantial gift to an academic program on the campus. "He made that contribution because initially our basketball team made him proud to be an alumnus of this college, which, in turn, reminded him of how much he had learned from the faculty in his major. He wanted to contribute to his academic program as a way of expressing his thanks for helping him become so successful in life." Jettisoning the football program, the athletic director said, would be shortsighted, especially since student participation in athletics is a much more complex endeavor than merely winning or losing.

I have to admit, I was similarly shortsighted several decades ago, when the university where I worked proposed creating a football team. We were in a state where, in any given year, you might find two or three football teams listed in the top 10 nationally.

Many professors on that campus thought it would be foolhardy to invest in a new football team to rival the other, highly competitive ones at public universities in the state. "Why not invest in raising faculty salaries?" some of us argued. "Or in student scholarships and postdoctoral fellowships?"

As it turned out, I was wrong. The university created the team, largely with private money, and it went on to become nationally competitive and the pride of many of us who had originally been skeptical. Far from draining money from academic programs, it helped bring cash into the university, not only in the form of direct revenue from events but also from auxiliary contracts—sales of memorabilia, fees for playing certain games, revenue from media companies, and the like.

Today, at the university where I am provost, some faculty members have made similar arguments: "Why not close the football team and reallocate the funding to academic programs?" And that sentiment is echoed at other institutions across the nation in these challenging economic times.

What my athletic-director friend found so frustrating about such discussions is that many factors are invisible to those unfamiliar with the overall workings of a university. Even a noncompetitive or "losing" team can help the university in multiple ways.

The mere fact of having a football team, for example, is often a plus for students thinking about enrolling. I've had students tell me that although they were not sports fans, they felt good about attending an institution that sponsored a football team. Perhaps it is because football and college life are so intertwined in the American psyche, but whatever the explanation, having a team can help recruit students, and having a winning team can help attract even better students.

Similarly, having an active athletics program, especially if it includes football, is often important to alumni. Even if the team is experiencing a poor year, the games themselves can evoke memories of when alumni were students, perhaps when the team was more successful. Having a team can help keep alumni engaged with the university, and, of course, a winning team can energize them. Those may seem like intangible benefits, but alumni are among an institution's greatest supporters, financially and otherwise. Keeping them engaged, even with a mediocre team, can have substantial payoffs.

The truth is, athletics events, especially football, are often key ways of attracting potential donors to contribute—and not just to the athletics program. When I served as a dean at another institution, I worked closely with donors who had allegiances both to athletics teams and to an academic program. Frequently those donors wanted to support both. I am certain that in many of those cases, we might not have been successful in interesting the donors to give to academic programs were they not first interested in athletics.

Sports teams can foster a deep sense of community and social solidarity, even when those teams lose more often than they win. One alumna told me that she would "never give up" on her team.

Most important, athletics can increase access to higher education for some students who might not have had the financial ability to attend college were it not for athletics scholarships and other aid. And, of course, the discipline and perseverance that a student learns from participating in sports are skills essential to mastering intellectual work as well.

Rather than pitting athletics against academics, what is needed is close collaboration between the two. I was exceedingly impressed with the approach of one athletic director I know. An institution where I once worked had just hired him, and one of his first actions was to request a meeting with the provost, deans, and other academic leaders.

At the meeting, he assured us all that he saw athletics and academic programs as close partners, and that his own success would be linked in part to the academic success of his student-athletes. He then proceeded to make clear to all athletes that he expected them to excel in their studies as well as on the field.

Those of us on the academic side of the house did our part as well—making sure that the athletes had access to academic-support services, such as peer mentors, tutorial programs, and writing and math centers. In some cases, we shared the costs of those services. The collaboration resulted in academically stronger students and more-disciplined athletes.

That athletic director's attitude is certainly a long way from what we often found in the bad old days, when coaches would sometimes attempt to intimidate or bribe faculty members (often with choice tickets to games) to overlook athletes' excessive absences or to be especially lenient with grades.

The point is that athletics and academic programs can—and should—work together for the greater benefit of students. Far from a drain on the academic endeavor, athletics can be the perfect complement, both through increasing community and alumni support and through adding disciplined, hard-working students to the institution's overall population.

I am not suggesting that institutions like Hofstra have made a mistake in eliminating football or other programs. Every institution must assess that decision in the context of its own campus. But what is clear is that often there is more than meets the eye when it comes to making such decisions. The one certainty is that athletics and academic programs should not be seen as somehow working against one another.

❖ ❖ ❖

How Not to Reform Humanities Scholarship

The Modern Language Association—the principal organization representing the disciplines of English and foreign languages—held its annual convention in January, and while the event was in session, I received calls from a handful of deans and department chairs. They were concerned about a trend they found alarming: the growing number of commentators there who were recommending changes in how the discipline conceives scholarly work.

Such recommendations, my callers unanimously agreed, would damage not only the careers of aspiring and new professors but also the reputation of the humanities. The proposed changes would also present substantial challenges to academic administrators charged with evaluating scholarship for tenure and promotion.

Among other things, the reforms call for replacing the traditional monograph-style dissertation with alternative types of final projects; reconceiving professional scholarship to be less dependent on traditional forms and standard scholarly venues; and moving more toward open-access dissemination of scholarship. The proposals are similar to measures being considered by other disciplines in the humanities. I agree with my callers: Considered from intellectual, political, and administrative perspectives, the proposals are wrongheaded and ill-timed.

The reasons given for the changes vary. The proposal to allow dissertators to submit alternative projects in place of a standard humanities dissertation arises from a widespread sense among faculty that the time to completion for the doctorate in humanities disciplines has become intolerably long—an average of nine years, by some accounts. In addition, the scholarly monograph is increasingly considered to be an endangered species, principally because publishers are finding it difficult to sell those works and are publishing fewer of them every year.

While flexibility is certainly called for, a rush to jettison the monograph-style dissertation could have several negative implications. Some veteran faculty members worry that graduate students and young faculty members—all members of the fast-paced digital world—are losing their capacity to produce long, in-depth, sustained projects (such as monographs).

Many scholars have made a similar point. Maryanne Wolf, a cognitive neuroscientist at Tufts University, makes a cogent case in her book, *Proust and the Squid: The Story and Science of the Reading Brain,* that one disadvantage of the digital age is that humans are rapidly losing their capacity for deep concentration—the type of cognitive absorption essential to close, meditative reading and to sustained, richly complex writing. That loss is especially deleterious to humanities scholars, whose entire occupation depends on that very level of cognitive concentration that now is so endangered.

Learning to produce a traditional monograph-style dissertation, then, is essential training for a humanities scholar these days because the experience helps neophyte scholars overcome the cultural and cognitive sway of attention deficit to which we are all prone now.

Besides, the typical rationale for abandoning the traditional dissertation—that the time-to-degree for the humanities doctorate is too long—is not a function of the monograph as a genre; it is a function of some dissertators' personal lives, as they attempt to juggle numerous priorities along with completing a dissertation. What's more, allowing doctoral students to produce alternative projects may well disadvantage them on the job market, as hiring committees—or at least some members of them—may not be as receptive to experimental forms and may favor candidates who have, in fact, produced a monograph.

The proposals to reconceive scholarship to be less dependent on traditional forms and venues and to move more toward open-access dissemination of scholarship also present problems. In effect, those two proposals are advocating a move to "digital scholarship" in all its many forms: online journals, Web sites dedicated to scholarly subjects, and publication of scholarly works on the Internet available to anyone who wishes to access them, among other forms.

I certainly understand how the new digital forms of presenting scholarship may be more attractive to some scholars than the traditional formats. The immediacy of the Internet provides instant gratification to those who wish to see their work publicized. However, offsetting the positive aspects are several disadvantages. As the administrators who called me from the MLA convention pointed out, the new approaches would make the job of evaluating scholarship almost impossible and would put some scholars at a disadvantage in the hiring-and-promotion process.

Advocates of the reforms usually say things like "there are many ways to share scholarship with colleagues" or "the present system is clunky and delays a scholar's ability to share his or her research with the field." That language of sharing, however, simplifies the scholarly enterprise.

Scholarship is not simply about "sharing"—about disseminating research results. It's about publishing work that has been appropriately vetted by responsible experts in the area of study so that readers can approach the work with a reasonable expectation that it was well conceived, proficiently executed, and, therefore, potentially useful to other scholars.

Even before the digital age, scholars shared their prepublished work with colleagues, usually by passing around photocopies. But sharing and publishing mean very different things. Can you imagine if the *Journal of the American Medical Association* (the paragon of peer review) were to decide that rigorous review of medical research was no longer necessary and that all researchers need do is make their latest work available online?

Most scholars in the medical fields (not to mention the public at large) would consider that an unacceptable lowering of standards that could very well lead to serious consequences for public health were doctors to follow ill-advised procedures that they read online but that had not been properly scrutinized. Why should humanities scholars settle for lower standards for their own disciplines?

The linchpin of the process of producing and disseminating scholarship is peer review. It is what distinguishes the professional scholar publishing serious research results from the amateur or dilettante simply posting thoughts online. The first likely underwent substantial scrutiny; the latter likely did not.

It is true that more and more online journals are claiming to employ a peer-review process. That could be a positive development if we can arrive at a point where the community of scholars has confidence that the review process in online venues is as rigorous as it is in top-tier print journals. At the present, however, many scholars are still skeptical that the processes are equivalent. Consequently, scholars who rely solely on electronic venues to publish their scholarship run the risk that members of hiring or promotion committees will devalue or discount the works.

My callers from MLA were especially concerned about that. "I can just imagine how my colleagues in our very traditional department would respond to a colleague's tenure application if most of the work were digital," said one department chair. "We would have a clash of cultures and values, and, sadly, I know who would win."

By far, the biggest concern of my callers was the political implications of the changes being proposed for the profession. Humanities scholars are embroiled in an intense debate over how to demonstrate to other academic disciplines and to society at large the relevance of the field. One of the criticisms of the humanities that I have heard for more than 30 years is that they lack rigor. A scientist recently said to me, "Philosophers and other humanists live the life of Riley: All they do is read and write all day."

It is precisely that perceived lack of rigor and meticulousness that causes critics of the humanities to assume that they are inferior disciplines and therefore expendable, especially during state fiscal crises. That is why the types of measures being proposed are extremely ill-timed. The move away from the traditional dissertation will be perceived by some critics to be a degradation of the Ph.D., and the move away from traditional schol-arly forms and venues without corresponding measures to certify a rigorous system of peer review is in place will be read as an erosion of standards. Those perceptions—valid or not—are ones we can ill afford at a time when every humanities discipline is experiencing frontal attacks from within their own institutions as well as from state legislatures and governors.

I am not against change, nor are the colleagues who called me. We're not trying to protect the status quo. We're trying to keep new and aspiring colleagues from making choices that might damage their careers, at least until more consensus can be established within the disciplines. And we're trying to protect the reputation of the humanities.

"These proposals are a prescription for our own demise," one caller told me. "I hope we can find a way to accommodate the new digital forms while demonstrating to everyone the high quality of humanities scholarship." I couldn't agree more.

4

Faculty Concerns

♦

The Limit of Academic Freedom

In the summer of 2009, I wrote a column attempting to clarify the meaning of shared governance (*The Chronicle*, July 24, 2009). Since then, some readers have requested that I do the same for academic freedom.

It's a particularly timely request, given that the American Association of University Professors recently announced a campaign to enhance academic freedom at public universities.

Most of us in academe cherish the protections afforded by academic freedom, but too many are unclear as to its limits. I have known colleagues who believed that academic freedom allows them to say anything they want, to anyone, in any venue, or to engage in behavior that most observers would assume to be inappropriate in any other workplace.

In fact, academic freedom has been claimed as an excuse for the most abusive and uncollegial behavior—shouting at colleagues, publicly berating students or staff members, defaming supervisors or other university administrators, shirking professional duties. One colleague even told me that academic freedom would protect her even if she indulged in slander and character assassination. "So long as you believe that what you are saying is the truth," she said, "then you are fully protected by academic freedom." (Needless to say, what a person "believes" is hardly an appropriate defense for violating a law.)

Department heads have told me countless stories of how academic freedom has become the generic excuse for any number of irresponsible acts. One chair described a senior professor who missed a substantial number of her classes. When confronted with evidence of her absenteeism, she told her chair that as an academic she had the freedom to conduct her courses in any way she deemed appropriate.

"I tried to explain that as an employee she has certain contractual obligations and that academic freedom did not free her from those responsibilities," the department head explained. "But it took the dean and, finally, the provost to convince her that not only did she have no such freedom but that she would be jeopardizing her future employment if her absenteeism persisted."

Another department head said one of her professors managed to avoid teaching his course the entire quarter by assigning a graduate research assistant to "facilitate discussions." The professor never showed up in class after the first day. In effect, the graduate student was forced to teach the course in addition to carrying out her research duties. When undergraduates brought the situation to the department head's attention, the professor angrily insisted he was protected by academic freedom and threatened to sue if the chair pursued the issue.

I know of yet another incident in which a fistfight erupted between two colleagues at a faculty meeting, resulting in bruises and a bloody nose. Both later contended during a formal hearing that they were "covered" by academic freedom and that the university had no recourse beyond reprimanding them for disrupting an official departmental meeting.

The practice of citing academic freedom to condone a limitless range of bad behavior has begun to take on the flavor of that hackneyed student excuse: The dog ate my paper (or, nowadays, My computer crashed). The magical incantation—"I'm protected by academic freedom"—is thought to offer instant indemnity. In reality, academic freedom, like tenure itself, is not a blanket protection.

The modern concept of academic freedom has two meanings. First, it refers to the right of an institution to manage its own curriculum and academic affairs without governmental interference. Colleges may determine, for example, what subject matter gets taught and who can teach it; establish their own admission criteria and graduation requirements; and develop their own academic mission and priorities. That is an important feature of American higher education. It establishes a crucial separation of power that discourages government from dictating that universities adopt particular positions or promote specific causes, and it prevents government from using educational institutions as part of a propaganda apparatus.

The second meaning of academic freedom involves the concept that faculty members may engage in research on controversial subjects (and, by extension, discuss those subjects in their classrooms) without fear of reprisal. This refers specifically to academic subjects and is not a blanket protection for any and all speech in any venue. As the AAUP's well-known statement on academic freedom cautions, professors "should be careful not to introduce into their teaching controversial matter which has no relation to their subject."

The distinction between speech related to one's discipline, on the one hand, and utterances about extra-disciplinary matters, on the other, is key to understanding academic freedom. Without the protections afforded by academic freedom, some scholars might fear for their jobs were they to challenge treasured assumptions in their fields, oppose well-established intellectual traditions, rewrite commonly accepted historical narratives, create artistic works that offend some sensibilities, or conduct scientific experiments that run counter to some people's ethical codes.

Academic freedom, then, facilitates scholarship and teaching by eliminating that concern over personal safety. Institutions benefit from the system because their faculty members may go on to produce groundbreaking work that brings greater distinction to the institutions. But a college or university has no comparable incentive to protect extra-disciplinary speech because such discourse is peripheral to the normal workings of the campus.

Because academic freedom is specifically intended to foster the free exchange of ideas within a community of scholars, it does not protect us from other types of utterances and behavior, such as slander or libel, bullying co-workers, lying on a *curriculum vitae*, or conducting one's classes in irresponsible ways.

The AAUP reminds us that as professors we are both private citizens and officers of our institutions. When speaking as citizens (perhaps at a political rally, say) we should be immune from being disciplined by the institution for our speech, but when speaking in our unique capacity as representatives of the institution—as scholars and teachers in our disciplines—we have an obligation to exercise caution in what we say and how we say it. In the latter role, according to the AAUP, our "special position in the community imposes special obligations" because our words are likely to be construed to represent the official position of the institution rather than our own personal views.

Some people confuse the constitutional concept of freedom of speech with the less grandiose notion of academic freedom, but they are two distinct concepts. Academic freedom is limited to the confines of academic discourse while free speech is a broad constitutional right central to our democratic system of government.

But even free speech has its limits. The constitutional right of free speech is not meant to protect each and every utterance regardless of context (yelling "fire" in a crowded theater when no such danger exists, engaging in "hate speech," or threatening a police officer). It is intended to protect you from being incarcerated by the state for expressing your views.

Academic freedom is a right we should all cherish because it ensures an environment of free inquiry. That is precisely why we must guard against attempts to make the concept so limitless, so capacious, that it loses its power to protect the academic enterprise. When academic freedom becomes all things to all people, then it becomes nothing at all.

❖   ❖   ❖

Exactly What Is "Shared Governance"?

At a recent conference of college administrators, several of us had an impromptu discussion over lunch about the meaning of "shared governance." The consensus? That term is often invoked but much misunderstood by both faculty members and many administrators.

"Some of my faculty believe that shared governance literally means that a committee votes on some new plan or proposal and that's it—it gets implemented," said a seasoned department head. "There is no sense of sharing, of who is sharing what with whom."

A dean chimed in that a faculty leader at her institution actually told her that shared governance means that professors, who are the "heart of the university," delegate the governance of their universities to administrators, whose role is to provide a support network for the faculty. "He said, in all seriousness, that faculty have the primary role of governing the university and that administrators are appointed to spare them from the more distasteful managerial labor," said the dean with incredulity.

That may be a more commonly held notion in academe than it at first appears. I know several faculty senators at one institution who regularly refer to faculty as "governance," as in "You're administration, and we're governance." That expression reveals a deep misunderstanding of the mechanism of shared governance—and presupposes an inherently adversarial relationship.

The phrase "shared governance" is so hackneyed that it is becoming what some linguists call an "empty" or "floating" signifier, a term so devoid of determinate meaning that it takes on whatever significance a particular speaker gives it at the moment. Once a term arrives at that point, it is essentially useless.

Shared governance is not a simple matter of committee consensus, or the faculty's engaging administrators to take on the dirty work, or any number of other common misconceptions. Shared governance is much more complex; it is a delicate balance between faculty and staff participation in planning and decision-making processes, on the one hand, and administrative accountability on the other.

The truth is that all legal authority in any university originates from one place and one place only: its governing board. Whether it is a private college created by a charter, or a public institution established by law or constitution, the legal right and obligation to exercise authority over an institution is vested in and flows from its board. Typically, the board then formally delegates authority over the day-to-day operation of the institution (often in an official "memorandum of delegation") to the president, who, in turn, may delegate authority over certain parts of university management to other university officials—for example, granting authority over academic personnel and programs to the provost as the chief academic officer, and so on.

Over time, the system of shared governance has evolved to include more and more representation in the decision-making process. The concept really came of age in the 1960s, when colleges began to liberalize many of their processes. In fact, an often-cited document on the subject, "Statement on Government of Colleges and Universities," was issued jointly by the American Association of University Professors, the American Council on Education, and the Association of Governing Boards of Universities and Colleges in the mid-60s. That statement attempted to affirm the importance of shared governance and state some common principles.

The fact that the primary organization championing faculty concerns, the body devoted to preparing future academic administrators, and the association promoting best practices in serving on governing boards together endorsed the statement illustrates that university governance is a collaborative venture.

"Shared" governance has come to connote two complementary and sometimes overlapping concepts: giving various groups of people a share in key decision-making processes, often through elected representation; and allowing certain groups to exercise primary responsibility for specific areas of decision making.

To illustrate the first notion of how shared governance works, I'd like to revisit a 2007 column, "But She Was Our Top Choice," in which I discussed the search process for academic administrators and attempted to explain why hiring committees are commonly asked to forward an unranked list of "acceptable" candidates. I wrote that shared governance, especially in the context of a search for a senior administrator, means that professors, staff members, and sometimes students have an opportunity to participate in the process—unlike the bad old days when a university official often would hire whomever he (and it was invariably a male) wanted, without consulting anyone.

"Shared" means that everyone has a role: The search committee evaluates applications, selects a shortlist of candidates, conducts preliminary interviews, contacts references, chooses a group of finalists to invite to campus, solicits input about the candidates from appropriate stakeholders, and determines which of the finalists are acceptable. Then it's up to the final decision maker, who is responsible for conducting background checks and entering into formal negotiations with the front-runner, and who is ultimately held responsible for the success (or failure) of the appointment.

"Shared" doesn't mean that every constituency gets to participate at every stage. Nor does it mean that any constituency exercises complete control over the process. A search cannot be a simple matter of a popular vote because someone must remain accountable for the final decision, and committees cannot be held accountable. Someone has to exercise due diligence and contact the front-runner's current and former supervisors to discover if there are any known skeletons that are likely to re-emerge. If I am the hiring authority and I appoint someone who embezzled money from a previous institution, I alone am responsible. No committee or group can be held responsible for such a lack of due diligence.

That's a good example of shared governance as it daily plays out in many areas of university decision making. No one person is arbitrarily making important decisions absent the advice of key constituents; nor is decision making simply a function of a group vote. The various stakeholders participate in well-defined parts of the process.

The second common, but overlapping, concept of shared governance is that certain constituencies are given primary responsibility over decision making in certain areas. A student senate, for example, might be given primary (but not total) responsibility for devising policies relevant to student governance. The most obvious example is that faculty members traditionally exercise primary responsibility over the curriculum. Because professors are the experts in their disciplines, they are the best equipped to determine degree requirements and all the intricacies of a complex university curriculum. That is fitting and proper.

But even in this second sense of shared governance—in which faculty members exercise a great deal of latitude over the curriculum—a committee vote is not the final word. In most universities, even curricular changes must be approved by an accountable officer: a dean or the university provost, and sometimes even the president. In still other institutions, the final approval rests with the board itself, as it does for many curricular decisions in my own university and state.

Clearly, when it comes to university governance, "shared" is a much more capacious concept than most people suspect. True shared governance attempts to balance maximum participation in decision making with clear accountability. That is a difficult balance to maintain, which may explain why the concept has become so fraught. Genuine shared governance gives voice (but not necessarily ultimate authority) to concerns common to all constituencies as well as to issues unique to specific groups.

The key to genuine shared governance is broad and unending communication. When various groups of people are kept in the loop and understand what developments are occurring within the university, and when they are invited to participate as true partners, the institution prospers. That, after all, is our common goal.

❖ ❖ ❖

When to Dissolve a Faculty Senate

The State Board of Education in Idaho—the governing board of all institutions of public education in the state—recently suspended my institution's Faculty Senate and directed the university's president to return in two months with a proposal for a reconstituted senate. I'll spare you the details as to why that unusual action was deemed necessary, since it concerns local politics, but it is, nonetheless, an occasion to reflect on such actions in general.

When the senate suspension was first announced, several commentators—including one reporter for a national publication—called the state board's action unprecedented. But it wasn't. Over the years, university boards or administrations (and occasionally faculty senates themselves) have elected to dissolve their senates and reconstitute new governance systems in their place.

In 1997, for example, the Board of Trustees of Francis Marion University dissolved the Faculty Senate and revoked its bylaws, replacing it with a new faculty governance system. The board's action was based in part on an accreditation report by the Southern Association of Schools and Colleges suggesting that in its incarnation at that time, the senate "tended to create an adversarial relationship between the faculty and administration, and between the faculty and the Board of Trustees."

Eight years later, the president of Texas A&M University at Kingsville suspended its Faculty Senate and created a new structure for faculty governance, accusing the senate of not cooperating with changes that were necessary to improve the university. In particular, the senate had opposed the president's efforts to increase the rigor of the institution's tenure-and-promotion process.

More recently, in 2007, the governing board of Rensselaer Polytechnic Institute suspended the Faculty Senate after its leaders rejected the board's demand that they amend the senate constitution to exclude non-tenure-track faculty members from its membership. The administration then created an interim faculty governance structure. The provost cited concerns about senate interference in an ongoing review of faculty governance as one reason for suspending the senate.

In some cases, governing boards have taken measures just short of outright suspension. In 2003, trustees at the University of Akron stripped the Faculty Senate of a number of key powers, such as having a say in the selection of deans, department chairs, and senior administrators. The board, responding to a faculty vote to unionize, also disbanded the senate's planning and budget committee and amended the rules governing financial crises. The trustees felt that those powers should be negotiated along with other issues on the bargaining table.

So the suspension of a faculty senate is not unheard of, but the reasons for it vary widely. At Francis Marion, it was an adversarial relationship between the faculty and administration. At Kingsville, it was opposition to change. At Rensselaer, it was the senate's rejection of a board directive. At Miami-Dade Community College, which disbanded its system of Faculty Senates in 1998, it was because the faculty voted to unionize. In a 2001 dispute at American University, it was an effort to provide a more "flexible, consultative, and efficient system of decision making."

One theme that recurs repeatedly in these disputes is the sense that faculty senates are working in opposition to the administration.

Take the University of the District of Columbia, for example. In 1992, trustees there dissolved the Faculty Senate, a 60-member body that was said to be obstructive, quarrelsome, and largely responsible for the university's "inadequate progress toward fulfilling its great potential." The university's president had criticized the senate leadership for attempting to interfere in administrative policy making and for being too closely aligned with the faculty labor union. Before the dissolution of the senate, the Middle States Association of Colleges and Schools had described it as adversarial rather than collegial.

Years later, in 2008, another president of the university again disbanded the senate and replaced it with an interim academic senate of department-elected faculty members. He cited the earlier senate's failure to carry out its responsibilities as part of the university's overall system of governance. Each side would, no doubt, offer a different explanation of what went wrong, but clearly, a pattern of contentious relations dominated the relationship between the senate and the administration.

Another common allegation in these disputes is that a senate has impeded progress on the campus, either because of a bloated committee structure or because of intentional delays of proposals it finds distasteful.

Of course, not all changes in governance occur because of adversarial politics. Most institutions change their governance systems in more amicable, collegial circumstances. Typically, that takes one of two forms. Sometimes, separate advisory groups unite to form a new governing body, often called a University Senate or an Academic Senate. At other times, the constituent groups within a single senate elect to dissolve and form separate governance groups (such as a staff council, a student senate, and a faculty senate).

Wichita State University, for example, dissolved its University Senate in 1993 and created four separate senates—one each for faculty members, students, classified staff members, and non-classified staff members. In 2000, the trustees of the College of New Jersey instituted a new governance system that included separate bodies for faculty members, staff, and students, but within a single integrated committee structure designed to allow people to make recommendations in their principal areas of responsibility. According to an internal document, the college's previous system was "complex, overly formal, and marginalized some campus stake-holder groups."

In a unique twist on the theme, the University of Notre Dame's Faculty Senate voted in 2001 to dissolve itself, contending that the senate had no real power or influence over university decision making. The senators were frustrated with the senate's advisory-only role. The senate later reversed its vote.

Clearly, over the years universities have dissolved and reconstituted their governance structures for a variety of reasons and circumstances. But in all of those cases, one or more of the participants cited the need for an improved governance system—one that was more efficient, more cooperative, more representative, more responsive, or more capable of accommodating change.

The most efficient, productive, and collegial model that I have experienced is one in which the senate chair and the chief academic officer jointly set the agenda for each senate meeting. They work collaboratively to conduct the meetings and deliberate on proposed policies and procedures.

Perhaps American University can serve as a good example for institutions seeking to embrace the values that enhance shared governance while operating in an efficient manner.

In 2001, the president replaced a universitywide senate with a smaller faculty senate that would focus on academic and faculty issues and provide advice on potential administrative decisions. According to the university's self-study prepared for the Middle States Association Commission on Higher Education, the new governance structure was built on four principles: that a governance system should be democratic and inclusive; that faculty time is valuable; that decisions should be made on the local level whenever possible; and that duplication of efforts and functions should be avoided.

It seems to me that American University has got it right. To be effective and legitimate, faculty governance must be both inclusive and democratic. To be efficient, it must be streamlined to avoid squandering faculty time and effort, and it should not duplicate or trump the efforts of faculty governance bodies on the local level.

More than any other factor, the key to establishing an efficient, productive governance body is mutual trust and understanding. All sides must understand that they are partners in helping to move the institution forward, not adversaries. It is when the parties lose sight of that key dynamic that the relationship can go very wrong.

❖   ❖   ❖

It *Is* Who You Know, And Who Knows You

As provost, I write a weekly column for a local newspaper highlighting the research of my university's faculty and familiarizing readers with our key academic programs. Recently, a faculty member contacted me and sheepishly suggested that in a future column I might want to write about the research he and his colleagues were doing.

He apologized repeatedly for what he called "shameless self-promotion," but he was rightly proud of his groundbreaking work and eager for others to hear about it. "I know you have more important subjects to write about," he said. "But I thought that news of our work might make more people proud of the university."

I was momentarily struck by the timidity of this otherwise self-confident man. But then I was reminded of an odd paradox of academic life: Faculty members are expected to become world renowned in their disciplines and well respected within their institutions, yet are also expected to avoid appearing to be self-promoting or, worse, boastful. In fact, many professors over correct by adopting a false humility—feigning, for example, not to want a particular award, honor, or position when the exact opposite is the case.

Apparently, this stance is so much a part of our collective DNA that it begins even before we become faculty members. Learning to network early in your career is one way to increase the likelihood that you will be successful in academe. I routinely advise new scholars that networking—forming professional relationships with other scholars in a field—is an important way to help build their credentials. I have spent three decades serving as a mentor for doctoral students and junior faculty members, and yet I am continually surprised to hear them dismiss networking as a clear form of self-promotion.

At workshops when I mention networking, someone inevitably blurts out, "Aha! Just as I thought: It's who you know that counts!" The implication is that, somehow, that system is corrupt and people are rewarded or advanced based principally on favoritism and personal relationships, not on intrinsic merit.

My standard reply is, "Of course it's who you know. How could it be otherwise? If no one knows you exist, how can you expect you and your work to be 'known'? Networking is the way you become known, and recognized, in your discipline."

Clearly, some people have confused the important work of promoting your ideas and research with a kind of fatuous promotion of self. Promoting yourself ("Look how great I am") is different from promoting your scholarship ("Here's what my research has discovered" or "Here's what I've been working on lately"). Central to the research endeavor is the desire to disseminate the results of your scholarship widely, and while interesting or groundbreaking research will certainly reflect well on the researcher, the focus should be on the former.

I know one prominent scholar whose narcissism is legendary. You would be hard pressed to carry on even a brief conversation with him without his reminding you of his importance. That is the type of behavior that is objectionable because his main subject of discussion always seems to be himself and only secondarily his work.

By contrast, I know plenty of equally prominent scholars who are quick to tell you about their recent research but do so without focusing relentlessly on themselves.

A long-serving dean once told me, "The small handful of faculty who behave like used-car salesmen ruin things for all the rest." As a dean, part of her job is to publicize the accomplishments of her faculty because the more people who are aware of and impressed with them, the more successful she will be in attracting donors to support the college. She needs professors to help her get the word out about their accomplishments, and not be shy or reticent about their work. But she's found that some faculty members are reluctant to talk about their research publicly because they do not want to be likened to those few boastful colleagues.

New faculty members make a critical mistake when they go so far to avoid appearing full of themselves that they skip opportunities to network or to describe their research to others. Professional conferences, for example, present ideal opportunities for emerging scholars to develop the types of relationships that will help them build their credentials. Here are some common ways that new faculty members might begin to make themselves known in their disciplines:

Introduce yourself. After hearing an especially good conference presentation or one that is relevant to your own strand
of research, go up and meet the presenter. It's a simple way to
begin building professional relationships with fellow scholars.
Occasionally, these short introductions turn into substantive discussions about common research interests. I have even witnessed
such a chat result in the presenter's inviting the young scholar
to contribute to a edited volume, join a research project, or
participate in a panel presentation.

Talk to editors. Introduce yourself to the key journal editors
and book publishers in your discipline. They play a pivotal role
in who and what gets published, and it is best when they can
associate a face with a manuscript.

Offer to serve as a manuscript reviewer. Not only is that good
experience, it also helps you stay current in your field because
you are reading the most recent research well before it is published. A bonus is that if you earn a reputation with journal
editors as a thoughtful and judicious reviewer, they will be more
likely to trust your judgment when you submit your own manuscript. You might also approach a journal editor and offer to
contribute a review of a new scholarly book. Especially if you
have not yet published your own research, writing a book review
is an excellent way to break into print.

Volunteer to review conference proposals. Contact the orga-
nizer of a professional conference in your discipline and offer
to serve as a proposal reviewer. As with manuscript reviewing,
this is a superb way to remain current with the latest research
while building valuable professional relationships.

Make friends in your disciplinary society. Introduce yourself to officers of your professional organization and ask how
you might become more involved in the organization (chairing
important committees or running for election to the executive
board, for example).

While networking is how your peers learn about you and your work,
it is in your interest that people outside the campus are aware of it, too.

The dean I mentioned who was frustrated by her faculty's reluctance to help publicize their research was attempting to use local and regional news media to familiarize the public with her faculty's accomplishments and lay the groundwork for effective fund raising. Here are some tips so that you as a faculty member can help in the effort:

> **Inform your department chair first.** Always let your department head know of your recent accomplishments. The chair should be at the forefront of publicizing faculty accomplishments to the institution and beyond.

> **Keep your media liaison informed.** If your institution has a well-developed advancement operation, then each department will have a designated liaison responsible for passing on news of faculty accomplishments to the institution's public-relations department. The professionals there will then notify the appropriate news media. Always let your liaison know when you win awards, secure important grants, or have other accomplishments that will reflect well on the institution.

> **Or talk directly with the public-relations office.** If your institution does not have an advancement liaison, then you can always pass on news directly to PR. Most universities publish faculty accomplishments in an internal newsletter and select certain accomplishments for even wider coverage.

Sure a few academicians go too far in the self-promotion department. But being too shy may well hold back your progress in becoming a player in the discipline.

In short, it is who you know (and who knows you) that counts—but that's a good thing.

Creating a Culture of Recognition

Every year at my university's annual celebration of distinguished alumni, inevitably it becomes clear that one or more of the handful of honorees has studied under the same senior scholar: a now retired professor of biological sciences. His students have been remarkably successful, carving out impressive careers in scientific research, medicine, and teaching.

At this year's celebration, I playfully asked him, "Is there any former student of yours who *hasn't* gone on to win some major award?" Immediately, his face darkened and he replied solemnly, "You know, I'm afraid that I'll pass away before all the truly worthy ones receive the recognition they deserve."

It strikes me that this emeritus professor understands a fundamental dynamic of academic life that many of us have yet to learn: The true cultural capital on any campus is proper recognition of good work.

Ours is an economy of scarcity. Even well-endowed institutions find themselves in a constant struggle to find enough money to do everything they want to do. That economy of scarcity extends to salaries: most academics and administrators are not compensated at the level that their education, skills, and experience would garner in business or industry.

In the absence of sufficient real capital, the cultural capital of the academic world—recognition—is especially important. We live for—and thrive on (whether we admit it to ourselves or not)—the recognition of our colleagues, peers, disciplines, and institutions. Strangely enough, however, institutions can be stingy when it comes to handing out praise. At times, it seems scarcer than dollars.

That is especially unfortunate because the longer someone's outstanding efforts go unacknowledged, the more that person is likely to become alienated.

A department secretary once told me that staff members in her unit were "banned" from attending department meetings, as if they were children not yet mature enough to join their parents at the dinner table. "Do they actually think that we're not part of this department, too?" she asked me in frustration. "I've been in this department longer than just about every single professor."

Although the staff professionals in her department work tirelessly to keep the unit running smoothly—including taking on such high-level responsibilities as managing the budget and the course schedule—they receive very little recognition of that "invisible" labor. So, they are understandably resentful.

A senior professor at a large public university told me a similar story. She felt ignored, even disrespected, by her colleagues despite making every effort to become a more integral part of her department. Eventually she abandoned all attempts to "join" her department and, for 26 long years, hunkered down and concentrated on her research, producing groundbreaking scholarship. Despite her fame, her departmental colleagues continued to dismiss her accomplishments. It was only when her university conferred on her the status of "university distinguished professor" that she felt part of the institution—a full quarter of a century after she began her career there.

Such stories are all too common in academe, and they illustrate a systemic problem. Researchers revealed last month one reason for the behavior of a significant number of university scientists (33 percent) who had admitted in a survey to knowingly engaging in research misconduct, such as falsifying data. The scientists perceived themselves to be victims of injustice, usually involving how their universities recognized and rewarded faculty work (*The Chronicle*, April 7, 2006).

Like the long-ignored professor and the staff members banned from their own department's meetings, those scientists felt that the institution—their colleagues and administration—had slighted them by not acknowledging their worth and by not adequately rewarding their efforts. The survey results underscore just how deeply job disaffection can be felt by faculty and staff members, as well as the serious consequences that can arise from such discontent.

The good news is that an alienated labor force is not an intractable problem. Sure, it is unlikely that higher education will ever receive enough money to raise salaries to the point that faculty and staff members will feel adequately compensated, but an institution can do much to ameliorate the alienation that many experience daily.

The beginning of a solution lies with those of us who serve as administrators. The key, I believe, is to create a culture of recognition and reward.

Such a culture can take many forms. It involves recognizing, thanking, congratulating, and rewarding both faculty and staff members for their many accomplishments. It can be as simple as adopting the routine of sending an e-mail message or a personal note to individuals acknowledging their new publication, grant, award, or other achievement. It means notifying departmental and institutional newsletters and other publications of those accomplishments—and making sure that no one worthy of such attention is inadvertently excluded. It means announcing those accomplishments at appropriate public venues—department meetings, college addresses, convocations.

A culture of recognition means creating awards for all constituents: awards for outstanding teaching, research, and service; for notable staff and administrative service; for significant student achievements; for distinguished alumni; even for extraordinary departmental or collegial efforts (the department or college conducting the most successful fund-raising campaign, for example).

When possible, it also means memorializing that recognition by providing some tangible record of it: a plaque, a framed notice, a printed certificate, or some other commemorative inscription. It means sponsoring annual ceremonies where such awards can be presented and the winners publicly lauded and thanked.

It also means recognizing the efforts of those who labor behind the scenes: the secretary who works overtime to make sure the department's newsletter comes out on time, the staff member who organizes an event— even a ceremony honoring the accomplishments of others.

In short, a culture of recognition means being ever vigilant to people's accomplishments and taking every opportunity to acknowledge their efforts.

Of course, recognition is one thing; reward is another. The next step is to find ways to make the rewards as meaningful as possible.

A friend of mine at a midsized university is understandably proud that he created the institution's first "Provost's Award for Outstanding Teaching." That was clearly a positive initiative, but what he didn't see was that by attaching a measly $250 prize to the award he was unintentionally insulting his faculty members. He was, in effect, saying, "The university values good teaching, but only enough to give you a small token." And in so doing, he was demonstrating that the university didn't really value good teaching at all, or, more importantly, the efforts of those teachers it was supposedly lauding.

It would have been better to have offered no monetary prize than to have offered one so paltry.

Certainly, the number of awards that carry monetary prizes and the amount of those prizes will be a function of a given unit's fiscal health, but if creating a culture of recognition is a priority—as I believe it should be—then we ought to make every effort to make our awards as meaningful as possible.

What's more, academic leaders committed to fostering a culture of recognition will go beyond waiting passively to learn of the accomplishments of others so as to congratulate them. They will nominate worthy faculty and staff members for awards, citations, grants, fellowships, and other forms of support and recognition. They will stay abreast of their faculty members' work and what awards and other forms of recognition are available to honor that work, both within the institution and externally. They will ensure that the appropriate individuals receive information about those opportunities.

In short, they will make sure that their professors, staff members, and students apply for, and receive, the support and recognition they deserve. Such measures will not eliminate job alienation in academe; that would entail massive structural change. But creating a culture of recognition would do much to improve the climate and working conditions in higher education.

In an institution that had successfully created such a culture, no one would ever fear passing away before "all the truly worthy ones" had been recognized, because in a culture of recognition, no good deed goes unrecognized.

❖ ❖ ❖

How We Value Faculty Work

I attended a recent gathering for department chairs, and listened as the subject turned to how some faculty members misreport their accomplishments on their vitas and annual evaluation forms. "I have one professor who lists short pieces he writes for our departmental newsletter under his 'Publications,'" said one chair, "and another who counts coaching Little League as 'Service.'"

Do the faculty members mean to be misleading? Maybe, or maybe not. But the end result, the department heads agreed, was that some faculty members miscategorize their achievements or blur the lines between categories of work. That discussion led to a related subject: how universities value the various types of faculty work.

"Some of our colleagues," said one of the chairs, "are not clear on the usual hierarchy of academic values, especially when it comes to service and research."

Another chair added, "I'm sometimes amazed at the items that appear on a *curriculum vitae* and where they get listed." A third commented that some professors seem to believe that all activities have equal value. "We've got to do a much better job of mentoring our faculty," she concluded.

Most problematic, the group agreed, was how some academics conceptualize "service."

Of the three typical kinds of service—community service, institutional service, and service to the profession—the first one is the least valued in a university setting, and the last one is the most valued. Often, however, vitas and tenure cases do not clearly distinguish between those very different types of work.

Institutional service—chairing or serving on departmental, college, or university committees and councils—is the most easily understood. After all, it is a standard work assignment, the sort of task expected of every academic.

The confusion over service usually arises from a conflation of community and professional service.

The highest value lies in service to the discipline. Whether you are an editor of a scholarly journal, officer of your national professional organization, coordinator of a scholarly conference, manuscript reviewer for a press or journal, external reviewer for tenure and promotion, or contributor to the discipline in some other capacity, those activities typically receive the most credit in deliberations over tenure, promotion, and performance review.

Volunteering as a Boy Scout leader, serving as a museum docent, or working in a soup kitchen are all admirable and important contributions to society, but not the kind of service that universities give much credit for.

Giving a public talk at the local library on your area of expertise is an excellent way to enhance town-gown relations, but it is not equivalent to giving a talk to your peers at a major professional convention, where your talk (or at least your proposal) is likely to have undergone rigorous peer review. The two talks may even be on identical subjects, but one carries much more weight.

Similarly, giving a talk at your own institution is not the same as being invited to give a presentation at another university—unless, of course, the invitation at your home institution arose from some formal vetting process, as in a distinguished lecture series.

It's not that community service is insignificant. Certainly, civic engagement has become an important theme in higher education lately, and a positive one. The question is not whether we should pursue such projects in our courses or individually, it's how we report them to our supervisors.

Engaging in community-service projects might well say something about your character and your willingness to contribute to society, but it says little about your contributions to your students or your discipline—the two principal responsibilities of our profession, and our raison d'être.

Civic engagement can become a more valued activity if your project is specifically linked to the theme and content of a course you are teaching or research you are conducting. A good example: when a professor of social work organizes a class project around assisting residents of a local homeless center in order to demonstrate to the students how to apply concepts learned in class. Another example: when an adult-literacy specialist volunteers to tutor people in a local learning center while simultaneously gathering data for a research study on the efficacy for adult learners of certain pedagogical techniques.

Years ago I served as a volunteer in a private hospital for abused women, and while I employed techniques related to my work as a university English professor—teaching the patients how to keep journals, for example, that could later be used in group and individual therapy sessions—my work there had nothing to do with my teaching or scholarship. It played no role in deliberations over my tenure, promotion, annual evaluations, or merit pay rankings, nor should it have.

In fact, some institutions actively discourage faculty members from undertaking too much community service. A provost told me that when he was a dean at a fairly prestigious private college, the administration made it clear that community service would not count in faculty evaluations. "We wanted our faculty to focus on their research and, most importantly, on our students," he said. "We emphasized that their community work was their own business and that the college would not reward it."

Some professors also blur the lines in reporting on their research. A dean once told me that one of her faculty members actually listed editing his church's newsletter on his CV under the heading "Professional/Scholarly Activities."

"He contends that this work should count because he is an English professor and editing is something English professors do," she said, with amusement.

Another common blurring of lines occurs when professors lump all of their publications in one section of their CV without making any distinctions between those that were peer-reviewed and those that were not. I have seen faculty members list book reviews and opinion pieces published in the local newspaper under their "Publications" section, as if they were equivalent to peer-reviewed articles.

The chairs at the meeting I attended mentioned several similar bad practices:

- Listing items under "Books" that were not really books, such as pamphlets, study guides, and instructors' manuals;

- Not making clear whether a book or article you list on your CV is in print, in press, or under review; and

- Listing nonscholarly presentations (a talk before the Rotary club) along with scholarly presentations.

Other faculty members fail to make a distinction between contracted research and scholarly research.

A civil engineer who accepts a contract from the local city government to conduct research about improving traffic flow through a busy intersection might be employing her research skills, but such a project is a service to the community (and one for which she is compensated). It's not a contribution to the knowledge of civil engineering as a discipline.

While both activities have value, contributing to the knowledge base of one's field is substantially more important in the academic value system than helping the city solve a traffic problem.

Some professors may well pad their vitas intentionally. But most of the mistakes that professors make in reporting their work are probably the result of misunderstanding the hierarchy of academic values. You need only ask yourself one question: "To what extent does the activity or accomplishment contribute to the knowledge and progress of the discipline?"

Using that rubric, we can easily see that editing a scholarly journal trumps editing the neighborhood newsletter, organizing a scholarly conference beats organizing a school event, publishing a peer-reviewed scholarly monograph surpasses publishing an instructors' manual for a textbook, and publishing a peer-reviewed article reporting on scholarly research tops being paid to conduct research for a local company.

The key to reporting your accomplishments accurately is to remember academe's hierarchy of values.

❖ ❖ ❖

We Really Like You

Some decades ago when I was a new assistant professor at a major state university, a distinguished senior colleague explained to me how the tenure system worked.

"It's the old spaghetti method," he said. "You toss a few strands at the wall, and you see what sticks and what doesn't."

He went on to suggest that from the beginning the university only intended to give tenure to a fraction (he claimed a third) of the faculty members it had hired. Those who distinguished themselves would earn a place in the permanent professoriate; those who did not would move to lesser institutions—if they were lucky.

The university offered no formal support to those of us on the tenure track, much to our dismay. We were expected to absorb all of the academic street smarts we could on our own and, in effect, reinvent the wheel, or to find—again on our own—some mentor who could help us navigate the perilous waters of departmental politics as well as instruct us on how to achieve success in the discipline.

Some years later, an assistant professor of geology who was four years into her first academic position told me that she was leaving her large research university for a smaller institution that prided itself on its "friendly" atmosphere. She complained that she did not feel supported by her department or by the institution as a whole.

"I'm just another number," she told me, not bothering to conceal her resentment. "What happened to the community of intellectuals we were all supposedly joining?"

Those two incidents reveal an all-too-common institutional failure to guide, support, and thus retain faculty members. An institution will often invest considerable time, effort, and resources in recruiting new faculty members but then drop the ball when it comes to keeping them.

Successful retention means fostering a culture of support. It means, for example, protecting untenured faculty members from colleagues and departments that encourage them to take on an inordinately large service burden. It also means protecting them from overextending themselves through their own good will and eagerness to contribute.

A culture of support means offering effective mentoring programs. While some institutions have had success with programs that pair a senior professor with an untenured one, those efforts are rife with potential problems. Even when the pairings work, faculty members still need to feel that the institution as a whole supports them.

Perhaps better are programs that regularly convene untenured faculty members as a group to discuss tenure and promotion requirements, review methods of handling student complaints, learn about available resources (internal grant programs, teaching workshops, assistance with grant proposals or study-abroad applications), and address any other topic that comes up.

I believe that, as administrators, we have an ethical responsibility to guide new faculty members, and, as managers, we have a fiscal responsibility to do so. When an institution begins to lose young professors because they do not feel supported, someone is not doing his or her job.

A culture of support also means providing sufficient opportunities for new scholars to develop a peer-support network. Frequently, newcomers are introduced at an initial faculty meeting, and then are left on their own to meet people not only within their department but—perhaps more important—in other departments. Sponsoring receptions and other events for new faculty members throughout their first year or two enables them to develop peer relationships that can help them feel less isolated. Establishing such networks can be especially important to retaining female and minority scholars.

Some mentoring programs include a monthly informational session followed by a reception because the socializing that takes place is often more important than what happens during the formal session. Acquaintances formed early in a professor's career are often long-lasting and mutually supportive.

Finally, in a culture of support, faculty accomplishments are recognized and rewarded, especially publicly, through institutional newsletters, faculty meetings, college addresses, and convocations.

Fostering that culture begins as early as the recruitment process. A department chairman once bragged to me that he had managed to hire his department's first choice in a faculty search and to have gotten her at "the lowest end of the pay range possible." Somehow he believed that he was doing his department a service.

What he didn't understand is that by nickel-and-diming the neophyte instructor, he had already sown the seeds of resentment and job alienation before she had even arrived on campus. And as it turned out, the professor left after only two years and secured a position at a prestigious private college.

The department would have been better served had the chairman (and everyone else) worked to make the new hire feel wanted from the very beginning. Colleges that have been particularly successful in faculty recruitment treat every search—even for an entry-level faculty member—as if it were a search for a senior professor. That is, they understand that the key to recruitment is making candidates feel that the institution is genuinely interested in them at every step of the process. That same philosophy should permeate our retention efforts.

Of course, retaining faculty members is not only an issue at the assistant-professor rank. The loss of established scholars is sometimes even more consequential because they take with them years of experience, accomplishments, and institutional history. That is why some institutions have begun to offer a voluntary mentoring program that focuses on how newly tenured faculty members can begin the transition from junior to mid-career status.

For all faculty members, fostering a culture of support means more than providing moral support; occasionally it entails making every effort to come up with a suitable counteroffer when accomplished scholars are being wooed by other institutions.

A colleague once told me that her dean refused to match an offer from another institution that would have amounted to a $5,000 raise. Instead, the dean offered her $2,500—the exact amount that she would have received that year in the regular raise process and that she would have been ineligible for had she accepted the counteroffer. Instead, she left for the other institution, and her university lost a productive and nationally prominent scholar.

When an institution makes a genuine effort to retain a faculty member through a counteroffer, that effort affects more than the given professor. It sends a message to the entire department that the institution truly values excellence in teaching and scholarship, that faculty members who distinguish themselves (and thereby the institution) will be rewarded.

Conversely, when an institution makes only a token effort—when it attempts to "low ball" a scholar—it sends the opposite message: that good faculty members are expendable.

Some financially strapped institutions might find it difficult, if not impossible, to match a given offer. But when an institution can't quite match the salary, it sometimes can make up the difference with other inducements: research stipends, course releases, equipment budgets, and summer stipends, for example. An institution may not always be able to afford a given counteroffer, but making an earnest effort sends an important signal about its values.

Occasionally an institution will have trouble retaining faculty members despite every effort to develop a culture of support. That is why it is a good idea to conduct exit interviews with departing scholars. An exit interview might help administrators understand the root cause of a professor's decision to leave—low pay, a feeling that accomplishments were not recognized, a hostile environment in the department—and fix it to prevent other good scholars from moving.

In a true culture of support, no faculty member should ever feel like "just another number" whose career rose or fell according to "the spaghetti method" of evaluation.

❖ ❖ ❖

A Creature of Our Own Making

At this time of year, most institutions are completing their annual tenure and promotion cycles. Assistant professors are receiving letters congratulating them or, in some cases, informing them that they have to start looking for a new job. Undoubtedly, a collective sigh of relief will resound as another faculty cohort finally emerges from the dark years of anxiety on the track toward tenure.

Those six or seven probationary years seem fraught with worry. Untenured professors, regardless of their accomplishments, seem uniformly terrified until they hold in their hands that official letter conferring tenure. I have even known colleagues who had received congratulatory letters from both the provost and president but who refused to stop living in dread until they had received confirmation of their appointment from their university's trustees.

The pretenure years should be a time of excitement, growth, and professional maturation—not anxiety, stress, and fear. Faculty members deserve a culture of support, not neglect, during those crucial formative years, and institutions bear much of the responsibility for creating one.

It's not enough just to articulate and disseminate the university's tenure requirements, although that's a good first step. Institutions should establish programs for junior faculty members that demystify the process and mid-probationary tenure reviews that provide a comprehensive assessment of an individual's progress. They should also reassess the entire process periodically.

In fact, many institutions are examining their tenure processes and standards in light of a growing realization that the traditional tenure system is unnecessarily rigid:

- Some colleges are making policy changes to accommodate dual-career families raising children during the peak of their pretenure years, or single parents attempting to balance family life and progress toward tenure.

- Some institutions are offering alternative tenure clocks rather than forcing all faculty members through the same inflexible system.

- Others are providing opportunities to choose different ratios of teaching to research on which they will be evaluated.

- Not only has the Modern Language Association recommended a major overhaul of tenure standards, but even Yale University—that perennial bastion of high standards—is considering liberalizing its notoriously rigid system.

Institutions themselves can be a major cause of pretenure anxiety when they get bogged down in the specifics and lose sight of the big picture. Too often, a tenure committee will be so preoccupied with counting—numbers of published pages, publications, citations, and so on—that it forgets to ask the larger questions.

I've witnessed, for example, several departments' attempts to devise rankings of academic journals and university presses so as to introduce some measure of certainty and consistency to the decision-making process. Such attempts invariably fail because rarely will a given group of faculty members be able to arrive at a consensus over such ratings except, perhaps, of the most and least prestigious venues.

Whatever the institution's specific criteria, the tenure process is really about (or should be) making an assessment of the extent and quality of an individual's contribution to the institution and discipline, and the likelihood that that contribution will continue or even increase.

Certainly, numbers and rankings should play a role, but committees and administrators should also be making a holistic assessment of the candidate. Is the person a "good citizen" of both the department and the larger institution? Has the candidate demonstrated a consistent record of excellent teaching? Are both of those records likely to continue?

Critically important: Is the candidate "a player" in the discipline? Does he or she contribute regularly to the intellectual life of the discipline through research and service? Will the candidate continue to contribute and thereby bring distinction to the institution? (I suppose the ideal would be to have a faculty in which everyone is an award winner: Nobel Prizes, Pulitzers, Fields Medals, and the like.)

But more important than raw numbers is the record as a whole. And the profile of an "active contributor" will differ from discipline to discipline. Tenure candidates in audiology will look quite different from ones in chemistry. Audiologists would be expected to invest a substantial amount of time in clinical practice and supervision but not to produce the quantity of published research of the chemists, not to mention the number of external grants. So while numbers do tell us something, they are relative and paint a partial picture.

Administrators—especially deans and department heads—bear the greatest share of the burden in creating a culture of support.

First, we need to accept responsibility for keeping all faculty members well informed about tenure requirements and expectations. We need to guide young scholars, providing them with concrete strategies for satisfying those requirements and expectations, and monitoring their progress on an annual basis.

Perhaps as important, department heads themselves often need to be guided. I have witnessed numerous instances in which chairs ignored pretenured faculty members until right before they were set to apply for tenure. I've seen other chairs allow weak cases to go forward when they could have requested a one-year extension to give the candidate more time to strengthen the case.

In both scenarios, the department heads were negligent. Their role is to shepherd untenured faculty members through the entire process—not to wait on the sidelines as a detached observer.

That being said, they also need to exercise leadership. Recently, a fellow dean of arts and sciences complained to me about one of her department heads who had failed to make a hard decision in a tenure case. Although the candidate's record was appallingly deficient, the chairman wrote a glowing letter of support.

"He had absolutely no backbone," she told me. "He simply avoided all responsibility and sent the case forward to me and to the college tenure committee so that we would relieve him of the discomfort of making a hard decision. That's not leadership; it's cowardice!"

Leadership involves making every effort to help new scholars become successful, but it also entails exercising the courage to withdraw that support if, at the end of the day, a faculty member has not met the grade. Supporting an unworthy case erodes the department's credibility with the dean, the college committee, and the provost, thereby jeopardizing future cases.

Most important, it is manifestly unfair to those faculty members who worked hard, played by the rules, and produced a record consistent with institutional expectations.

I want to make it clear: I believe that numbers do matter. They provide a sense of accountability as well as consistency from case to case. But the enumeration of specific accomplishments should be balanced with a more general assessment of the candidate's contribution. We need both types of assessment.

The tenure system is a creature of our own making. It can be flexible, supple, and responsive to the diverse needs and life situations of faculty members, or it can be rigid, uncompromising, and so focused on the trees that it cannot see the forest.

The pretenure years need not be a time of high anxiety, but for that to happen, institutions will need to make structural changes in the tenure system. We will need to learn to ask of every tenure candidate, "Are you a player?"

❖　❖　❖

How Not to Measure Faculty Productivity

Measuring and managing faculty productivity has become one of the most significant and controversial policy issues in higher education, not only within universities but also within state governments.

A recent survey revealed that many chief financial officers in academe favor raising faculty teaching loads and eliminating tenure as key ways to better manage institutional resources. The governors of Texas and Florida have advocated for increased efforts to measure faculty productivity and to promote teaching at the expense of research. And this year Utah state lawmakers considered a bill that would eliminate tenure at the state's public universities and replace it with performance-based evaluation.

The most recent entry into the faculty productivity debates is a newly released report, "Literary Research: Costs and Impact," written by Mark Bauerlein, a professor of English at Emory University, and released by the Center for College Affordability and Productivity. The study's stated goal was to introduce empirical evidence to the discussions under way about faculty productivity in the humanities by examining the costs of research in four English departments and then juxtaposing those costs with the numbers of citations of works published by faculty members in those departments.

I agree that recent discussions about faculty productivity have been short of useful empirical data, but the center's study is deeply flawed and, therefore, contributes little to the debate. In fact, several of the mistaken assumptions made in the study are representative of misapprehensions repeated in other discussions on the subject.

Briefly, the study assumed that a third of a professor's salary is the amount the institution invests in that scholar's research. The study simply takes the department's salary budget, subtracts the salaries of lecturers, instructors, and creative writers, and excludes administrative and supplemental pay. A third of the remaining budget is deemed to be the department's total investment in research.

As might be expected, the study then determines that most of the works published by faculty members in the four departments were rarely cited in professional literature. The report's conclusion: Universities are squandering their money by supporting research that has "little consequence" when that money could be invested in teaching and other areas.

As with too many discussions of faculty productivity, the Bauerlein study does not look at the entire picture. If you are going to judge the relative worth of humanities research—or any research, for that matter—you have to examine the entire context.

An English department in a research university might employ 50 tenure-track faculty members—the most productive of whom have reduced course loads. But just adding up a third of their salaries gives you an incomplete picture. That same department might have 10 lecturers or instructors, all with expanded course loads. It may also have a large cadre of graduate teaching assistants, all teaching their own courses. If managed correctly by the department leadership and the dean, and monitored regularly by the provost, the collective course offerings of the department should be more than ample to cover its teaching obligations, which include the courses in its degree programs as well as its general-education requirements.

In a well-managed department at a research university, the faculty members typically have a variable course load, based on their research productivity. If the base-line standard load is teaching three courses a semester (as is the case at many universities), faculty members who are moderately productive in terms of their research might, in fact, have a "3-3 load" (teaching three courses each semester), while faculty members who are more productive in their scholarship would have a load of 2-3, 2-2, or less. Professors who have completely given up on research might be assigned a "4-4 load," or four courses each semester. The department's leadership has the obligation—often with the assistance of a faculty committee and established criteria—to make judgments about teaching assignments for a given academic year.

In effect, instructors, lecturers, graduate students, and nonresearch faculty members subsidize the reduced teaching schedule of productive, "research active" scholars. And, I might add, "research active" includes, in the case of English departments, those faculty members in creative writing, since their equivalent to research is the production of creative works. Arbitrarily omitting them from the assessment of departmental productivity, as Bauerlein did, further skews the evaluation.

What's more, a well-managed department will also continually monitor its curriculum to eliminate unnecessary course requirements and underperforming programs so as to ease the collective burden on the department. It will seek to keep its curricular commitments to the minimum necessary to serve its constituents well—but no more. Keeping unnecessary requirements and outdated programs on the books only adds to the collective workload.

The bottom line is that an efficient department is able to manage its curricular obligations while providing sufficient time for scholars to conduct their research and creative activities. Now Bauerlein might reply, "Yes, but if faculty were only teaching, then you could manage the entire enterprise for less money; you would no longer need to employ the lecturers and instructors." True. However, the assumption underlying that response and several of the recent discussions of faculty productivity is that the job of university professor is equivalent to the job of teacher, but that is simply not the case at a university.

As Bauerlein himself points out in his report, all you need to do is examine any university's faculty handbook or official tenure guidelines. You will find language that clearly specifies that, for promotion and tenure, faculty are expected to contribute to knowledge in their disciplines, usually in the form of publications or creative work. Bauerlein wants to dismiss the scholarship that is cited rarely, but that is shortsighted. A professor's research agenda—in the humanities or not—is typically a succession of studies in a given area. Works early in that succession might not receive as much attention as works completed later on in the process, but that does not make the earlier research "of little consequence." It may simply indicate that the earlier efforts are part of the larger project the researcher is working through.

Also, a simple citation count can be misleading. I can publish an article in which I make some outlandish claims, and that may well garner many citations as other scholars attempt to refute my statements. But someone else's article that attracts many fewer citations may actually be more useful to work in a particular subfield.

Besides, the research tradition in academe has always been to pursue knowledge for the sake of knowledge. Often a scholar has no obvious endpoint in mind when he or she embarks on a particular project but may unexpectedly make a monumental discovery.

We cannot predict ahead of time if someone's research project will be so important that it will win the Nobel Prize, or the Pulitzer Prize, so it would be counterproductive to determine in advance that scholars in any given area should not be conducting research and instead should be teaching more. That applies to every discipline, including those in the sciences.

Discussions of faculty productivity have got to become more sophisticated for this debate to lead to any sensible conclusions. Examinations of one aspect of productivity—independent of its larger context—are, well, of little consequence.

❖ ❖ ❖

Fight Your Own Battles

From time to time over the decades, I have witnessed what I consider to be one of the more disgraceful practices that we as academics can engage in: using students to further our own personal and political ends.

That dishonorable—not to mention unethical—practice takes many forms. It's mobilizing students to spread damaging gossip about a colleague. It's enlisting students in a campaign to unseat your department chair. It's encouraging them to contribute to a blog devoted to embarrassing the university's president. It's organizing them behind the scenes to write letters to the editor of your local or campus newspaper about a policy, colleague, or administrator you disagree with—and, in many cases, actually writing the letter for them.

A dean of liberal arts told me about one such incident in her college. A popular professor was denied tenure based on his weak record of scholarly productivity.

His department tenure-and-promotion committee had warned him in several successive annual evaluations that he was in danger of not making the grade and that he needed to ramp up his research activity. He had been counseled similarly by his department head.

The professor apparently did not listen and was denied tenure, with a letter informing him that he could continue working for the university for the coming year, but after that would no longer be on the payroll.

"He actually thought that he could pressure the university to reverse its decision," the dean told me. "He convinced his students to stage a protest on the quad, complete with placards and bullhorns. The students had been convinced that the university had done him some grave injustice, but they just didn't have the facts."

The dean explained that the protest petered out after a long weekend and had no effect on the tenure case, but by enlisting students in his personnel cause, the professor had succeeded in generating substantial ill will, both among his supporters and among those who supported the university's decision.

"It would have been understandable if the students had spontaneously chosen to express their support," the dean added. "But the fact is that our disgruntled professor stage-managed the entire event, even to the extent of helping to paint protest signs."

I witnessed a different situation in which a professor was determined to destroy a rival in his department. He lobbied graduate students to avoid taking his rival's courses, and constantly told students stories about the rival's lack of support and sympathy for graduate students and his general unfitness to serve on the graduate faculty. Before long, the rival was unable to attract graduate students to his courses and was relegated to teaching undergraduates, despite the fact that he was a gifted graduate teacher. "It's unfair," the victimized professor told me. "If [the professor who engineered the attack] had a problem with me, he should have come and talked to me about it. Instead, I woke up one morning and found that the damage was done—all based on lies and innuendo!"

An extreme form of misuse of students for personal or political objectives is to enlist them to participate in academe's newest, and clearly its lowest, level of uncollegiality: mobbing. This is the practice of savaging a faculty member in a no-holds-barred onslaught from multiple colleagues.

Deans and department heads are reporting increased incidents in which faculty members have conscripted students to help in mobbing a professor. "It's a new nadir for the academy," one senior professor told me. "If we as a professoriate lose our collegiality, we lose our soul."

Perhaps equally reprehensible is organizing students to support your favorite political cause, whether in local or national politics. One research university was engaged in an impassioned debate over the ethics of animal research being conducted on the campus. A group of faculty members vehemently opposed all use of live animals in university research projects. Three of those professors organized a protest rally to be held, not on the campus, but on the steps of City Hall in the municipality where the institution was located.

While the organizers invited all faculty and staff members to participate, they concentrated on students, urging entire courses to descend on City Hall at the appointed hour. In several cases (and in direct violation of university policy), students were offered extra credit in their courses if they participated in the protest, regardless of the relevance of the course's subject matter to the issue of utilizing live animals in university research projects. The organizers were most interested in turning out large numbers of people and apparently had little regard for their own students.

Such efforts to "instrumentalize" students, to cast them as pawns in a political drama, are unprofessional and inappropriate on any number of levels. First, faculty members who use their students like that have lost sight of the fact that the power differential between students and professors makes the relationship inherently unequal. Our students may well be adults, but when a faculty member—especially one they respect—urges them to join a cause, they are in a precarious situation; their consent to participate can never be purely one of free will.

That unequal power relationship is not unlike that in romantic relationships between a student and faculty member. They both may be consenting adults, but the difference in power between them attenuates the student's ability to say "no" without complications.

So using students to aid in your own pet causes is deeply demeaning to students because it infantilizes them. It positions them as incapable of independent thought and asks them to act on behalf of "the one who knows better"—their surrogate parent, the professor.

What's more, that phenomenon is, in effect, a form of anti-intellectualism: careful consideration of the facts, reasoned debate, and a search for understanding and "the truth" are all sidelined in exchange for uninformed heated exchange and anonymity shielded by blogs and student surrogates.

It is, as well, an act of intellectual cowardice: When you hide behind your students, you never have to own up to your actions and positions given the cloak of anonymity they provide.

Interpersonal relationships can be difficult in any workplace, but we in academe supposedly have an advantage over those in other workplaces: We all have committed ourselves to the life of the mind, to careful investigation of facts, to faith in rational disputation, to critical thinking, to argumentation based on facts and evidence, and to collegiality. Deploying students as our surrogate warriors violates everything we stand for as a professoriate.

How to Run a Meeting

We all have experienced interminable meetings: the hourlong meeting to accomplish 10 minutes' worth of work, or the meeting that seems to have no purpose. Whether on the department level or the larger institutional level, inefficiently run meetings consume inordinate amounts of our time and energy.

That is worrisome, given how much of our academic lives we spend in committee work. The key difference between an efficiently run meeting and one that wastes time is whether we conceive of the committee as a structure to accomplish something concrete or as an occasion to fill time.

I know a department chairman, for example, who was notorious for running meetings simply to fill time. He never provided a printed agenda, either prior to the meeting or even when we arrived at the meeting itself. We typically would all assemble at the appointed hour, but rather than begin, he would spend 10 or more minutes chatting with everyone about mundane subjects.

Upon finally calling the meeting to order, he would amble through the subject matter with no apparent objective. The meeting would eventually devolve into a free-form discussion, devoid of structure or direction. By the time we actually got to the real work that needed to be done, most of an hour had elapsed, and we would then rush hastily through the actual work that we should have spent the entire hour focusing on. Because our decisions were made in haste, their quality was always questionable.

That same pattern would be repeated with every meeting that this chair moderated. It would be easy to blame the inefficiency purely on an incompetent chair, or one who was just bad at conducting a meeting. But what puzzled me is that several (but not all) of our colleagues tolerated—or even embraced—this practice. They seemed to enjoy the collegiality and the relaxed social nature of the meetings. It was as if they had no other work to do, or no other opportunities to socialize with their colleagues—neither of which was true.

A senior professor at a Midwestern university complained to me about how the graduate-program director in her department conducts his meetings. He apparently spends considerable time flirting with female committee members who happen to be junior faculty members or graduate students. "The constant pseudo-sexual banter is offensive enough," she said to me, "but so is the fact that he wastes my time with his nonsense, time I could be devoting to my research." She eventually asked to be removed from the committee.

Some committee chairs will insist on meeting even when there is no business to conduct. That often happens when a committee has a standing meeting time. I have even known chairs who began meetings by announcing, "We really don't have anything to do today, but let's touch base with one another." Obviously, such a practice shows a real lack of respect for people's time.

Other people convene a meeting and then fail to manage it. Rather than begin with clear goals, those committee chairs permit a kind of collective stream of consciousness to take over.

Still other chairs fail to control the behavior of committee members. In one department with which I am familiar, one professor would consistently seize control of departmental meetings and attempt to assert his own agenda. The meeting would rapidly spin out of control, but the department chair would do little to steer the group back to the task at hand. In a few instances, the sessions degenerated into shouting matches.

And, of course, sometimes committee chairs will run meetings poorly on purpose. For example, occasionally a chair will deliberately take a leisurely or even tedious pace through a meeting, hoping to wear down the committee members so that when they finally do arrive at an issue of substance, they will hastily approve the proposal just to end the meeting. That is a time-honored strategy for steering a controversial measure through the approval process, but it, too, does a disservice to busy colleagues, not to mention being dishonest.

Clearly, meetings in a professional setting are not opportunities to socialize or to fill time aimlessly; they are instruments for conducting business. Academics are busy people, and it is not only a disservice but even a form of disrespect to squander our time. That's why conducting committee work in as efficient a way as possible is a mark of collegiality and respect. Here are some best practices for running meetings efficiently.

- Cancel a meeting if you have a light agenda. Better to have a fuller agenda at the next regularly scheduled session than to ask colleagues to meet with little to do. Remember: It takes time to prepare for and arrive at a meeting, and that, too, is valuable time.

- Hand out an agenda in advance of the meeting. A published agenda helps everyone stay on track.

- Always limit the length of a meeting and monitor the time so that it doesn't go on too long. For example, don't schedule an hour meeting if the tasks at hand can reasonably be accomplished in a half-hour.

- When appropriate, pass out supporting documents in advance so that people can arrive prepared. The better prepared that committee members are, the more likely they are to work efficiently.

- Begin every meeting on time, not 10 minutes late. That practice is a sign of respect for committee members' time, and it cuts down on the likelihood of rushing through part of the agenda later. (And once members know that you will always begin punctually, they will be more likely to show up on time.)

- Immediately after calling a meeting to order, make clear the purpose and objectives of the session: "We need to make three key decisions this morning." The best committee chair is goal oriented and guides the group from task to task.

- Establish guidelines for members' participation and behavior. For example: "Members will be expected to limit their contributions to a discussion to no longer than two minutes at a time; no one member will be allowed to filibuster or monopolize." Or, "Members will be expected to adhere to the topic at hand and not lead the discussion off to other subjects."

- Use e-mail to conduct minor committee work so as to save face-to-face time for more important tasks.

- Conduct your meeting not only efficiently but fairly. Steam-rolling through the decision-making process without providing adequate time for discussion and deliberation does not equate to efficiency.

Another form of inefficiency is when a department or college creates two or three committees when a single panel could easily handle the workload. Some departments have established an astounding number of committees. It is always in a department's best interest, whenever possible, to consolidate the workload into fewer committees so as not to overburden its faculty and staff members.

Many colleges, for example, have established a committee on tenure and promotion, another on budget recommendations, a third on personnel matters, such as hiring priorities, and a fourth on allocation of laboratory and classroom space. Increasingly, colleges are consolidating the work of all four into one panel, often called an "executive committee," and providing some form of compensation for committee members (usually release time from teaching) because they are taking on a high workload.

The advantage of the supercommittee system is easy to see. The workload of four committees might have been spread among 20 or 25 faculty members, some doing double duty on more than one committee. But with a single panel, six or seven faculty members can carry the load, freeing their colleagues' time for research and teaching.

Whether it is because of inefficiently run committee meetings or because a department or college has been injudicious in how it has established its committee structure, we all risk wasting too much time in committee work. Like it or not, such service constitutes a substantial part of every academic's workload. Doing it as effectively and efficiently as possible is a true act of collegiality.

5

Faculty Recruitment

♦

Don't Just Search, Recruit

A prominent athletics director once told me the secret to a successful college sports program: "What separates the consistent winners from all the rest is tenacious recruiting. A faithful alumni base and state-of-the-art equipment and facilities are all wonderful, but recruiting good people is the single most essential ingredient."

That is equally true of building a first-rate academic department. You may have shiny new facilities and cutting-edge technology, but nothing will bring a program to new levels of excellence faster and more effectively than attracting and retaining first-rate people. That is why searches for both professors and administrators are among the most consequential tasks we perform.

But savvy professionals in college athletics seem to understand what many of us on the academic side often do not—that "searching" and "recruiting" are not always the same thing.

Search committees sometimes assume they can simply place a job advertisement and sit back and wait to see which applicants emerge. It is almost as if we believe that actively pursuing candidates in the manner common to the business and sports worlds will somehow sully the rarified halls of academe.

Such passivity merely ensures mediocrity. If we are to build outstanding departments and colleges, we need to take a page from the athletics playbook and aggressively pursue the best and the brightest. Effective recruitment takes many forms and will depend on the context, but it begins with a search committee that has a clear understanding of its role in the process.

The committee's first objective is to entice top candidates to apply. That means selling the institution and the job as desirable, and it means undertaking a lot more work than some committee members may be prepared for, especially if their attitude is, "Well, if people really want the position, they will apply."

Committees aren't going to attract superior candidates by advertising in only one or two places. You might supplement your usual ads with notices in other, more specialized disciplinary forums and with announcements posted on electronic forums in the discipline.

For positions above entry-level, especially administrative ones, the committee might send personal letters inviting people to apply or to nominate others. That can be a costly enterprise because it usually entails purchasing a membership list from a disciplinary organization and incurring a hefty postage expense. Nevertheless, it is one of the most effective methods of developing a pool of good candidates, especially if the letters sent by your committee are written by someone the recipient knows personally or by reputation. Needless to say, those letters will be most effective if they appear to be genuine appeals and not form letters.

Ambitious committees should also arrange to make personal calls to a select number of potential candidates. A personal touch is particularly helpful in searches for senior faculty members and administrators.

Another option is to dispatch committee members or colleagues, armed with recruitment materials, to disciplinary conferences. Your ambassadors can disseminate information about the search and meet informally with interested parties to answer questions about the available position and the institution.

Publicizing the position in so many venues may seem redundant, but doing so ensures that the greatest number of people have the potential to see the announcement. Besides, some people may need more than one encounter with a job notice before entertaining the idea that the position might be a good fit for them. Seeing announcements in multiple forums may well convince them that the institution is serious about casting as wide a net as possible.

If the goal is to sell the position and institution to potential applicants, a Web site devoted to the search is a must.

Effective sites will contain more than a position statement and a list of committee members. The objective here is to make the site useful for the candidate, not the committee. The search site should contain links to sites that will best promote the institution and the community, so the key question to ask in constructing a site is, "If I were a first-time visitor to the institution, what information would help me understand what I might be getting into were I to accept a position here?" The search site can be an important recruitment tool, so it is wise to spend time planning and building it.

The search process is a supremely rhetorical situation. It entails determining your audience's needs and desires and devising a strategy to address them. As with any rhetorical occasion, it is important to put yourself in the place of the audience—the candidate. If it is true that the job search is a kind of courtship, then "recruiting" means wooing. Certainly, we all like to be courted, to feel wanted, so the objective of effective recruiting is to determine how to make each candidate feel desired.

I can't count the number of times I have witnessed a search destroyed because a committee member (or in some cases an entire committee) chose to transform the search from a courtship into an inquisition. You may derive a great deal of personal satisfaction from pummeling a candidate with a barrage of "tough" questions but that is a sure way to drive off an applicant. Also inappropriate is airing the department's dirty laundry during a campus visit.

Such behavior is self-destructive and unprofessional—and it happens all the time.

A courtship implies that both parties are looking one another over in an attempt to imagine what a long-term relationship might be like. A candidate who is given the red-carpet treatment during a campus visit is likely to develop positive feelings about the search process and the institution itself. Candidates who are badly treated will feel resentment even before an offer is tendered.

In one search I am familiar with, the organizers failed to arrange for individuals to escort candidates from one meeting to the next, and one candidate was even instructed to take the subway from her hotel to the university, even though she was unfamiliar with the city. (As luck would have it, she narrowly avoided being mugged on that ill-fated subway ride, and subsequently, had no hesitation in turning down a generous offer.)

And recruitment does not end once the finalists have visited the campus. Too often, a search committee will do a superb job up to that point and then drop the ball. It's like permitting the opposing team to rush in at the last minute and win the game even though you have been ahead from the beginning.

A provost I know once allowed a stellar dean candidate to slip through her fingers simply because she failed to understand that his original tepidly negative response to her offer was not his final word but was meant to be the first in what should have been a back-and-forth exchange. Instead, she politely thanked him for his interest in the institution and wished him well.

A skillful negotiator might have turned things around at that crucial point in the process. Rarely is an initial offer perfect—details will need to be ironed out, responsibilities clarified, understandings forged. What at first seemed unworkable might, in the end, have been salvageable.

When I extend an offer and the candidate responds, "I'm not quite sure this is a good fit," you can be certain that my first reply will not be, "Well, at least we tried." The response should be, "What can we do to make this work for you? Is there something creative we can do to make the position more acceptable?" Often, the accommodation a candidate needs is not costly or unreasonable but simply involves rethinking the details.

Over the years, I have hired several outstanding administrators who had turned down my original offer. Because I saw my task as "recruiting" the best possible individual, I was determined to do everything within reason to land the top choice. I was not about to take "no" lightly. If the goal truly is to build a great institution, then persistence, determination, and perseverance are not optional.

Search committees need not adopt all of these measures in every search, but the general principle remains the same: If building a first-rate academic unit is like developing a successful athletics program, then the search process is our one opportunity to assemble the ideal team. That means recognizing that passive searching isn't enough.

Why Settle for Second Best?

While conducting a search for a dean some years ago, I was astonished when a committee member urged me in confidence not to extend an offer to the candidate who had impressed even the toughest critics and who was clearly the first choice of the faculty and staff members.

The candidate was too ambitious, she said: "Some of us feel that he's too good for us and will leave us in four or five years for another university." The second-rated candidate was a "safer" choice though admittedly less dynamic than the charismatic frontrunner.

I have witnessed that identical scenario take place in searches on three other occasions at two universities. People in those searches claimed the institution wasn't good enough for the frontrunner and concluded that we might as well not bother tendering an offer. In another instance, I heard a faculty member sneer that her provost was not likely to remain at her campus for long, thanks to his "vaulting ambition." She saw him as so preoccupied with his career that he couldn't possibly care about the institution.

To me, those sentiments seem counterintuitive. The most outstanding dean I have ever served under accomplished more in his five-year tenure than many deans do in an entire career. He presided over a major restructuring of the college and created countless initiatives that moved the college in new and exciting directions.

When that dean announced he would be leaving to become provost at a considerably more prestigious institution than our own, I had mixed feelings. I would miss his leadership, but I was also proud—for him and for us. We had recruited a skilled and dynamic leader who had transformed the college in very positive ways, and now he was honoring us by going on to new and greater challenges. His success was our success. His move to a better institution confirmed that we had made a wise choice in hiring him.

The willingness to choose less-desirable candidates and disparage some for the "sin" of ambition all point to a striking difference between the academic and nonacademic worlds.

In nonacademic sectors, ambition is seen as a desirable attribute. Ambitious people are the ones most likely to take risks, work for change, and refuse to settle for the status quo. In the academic world, however, ambition is invariably seen as a defect, as falling prey to one's basest instincts, as being "career focused" rather than institution-focused.

In the nonacademic world, genuinely wanting a particular job is seen as an indicator that you will work hard to be successful once hired. In academe, revealing that you want a position will cause you to be looked upon with suspicion, as if you have some hidden agenda that could benefit only you and not the institution. In the end, it may even be the reason you were not selected for the position.

So, academics who want to make a mark in administration are forced to engage in a strange dance—feigning lack of interest in a position while working to persuade institutions that they are the perfect choice.

When I hire an academic leader, I want someone who is passionate about the job, who actually wants it. I want someone who has vision, the skill to communicate it to others, and the ability to convince them to buy into it so thoroughly as to make it their own. I want an academic leader as opposed to simply an administrator.

I want someone who is ambitious. And, yes, I would like that candidate to remain in office for a reasonable length of time, especially since we will have invested substantial time and resources in recruiting that person. But that is by no means my paramount selection criterion.

Academics who appear ambitious are accused of being concerned primarily with their vitas, but what's wrong with that? Since when is caring about one's career necessarily in opposition to doing a good job for the institution? From the neophyte assistant professor to the seasoned university professor, we all have career aspirations, however modest. Not only is that not a bad thing, it is healthy. The mistake is to assume that having career goals is somehow inconsistent with performing your job well and acting in the best interest of the institution.

More often than not, the two are interdependent: The accomplishments noteworthy enough to advance your career are likely to be the very initiatives that help move your college forward.

Those who choose the supposedly "safe" candidates have it backwards. The primary goal of an administrator who is truly careerist is to remain in the job while not alienating too many people (presumably to facilitate smooth sailing to the next job). Their strategy: Proffer no vision, assume no risk, attempt no change, make no tough decision that will cause some group or another to oppose you.

In a very real sense, then, the genuinely careerist person is the do-nothing administrator, not the "ambitious" one.

Perhaps what really lies behind the kind of institutional diffidence that would cause someone to hire the inferior candidate is fear of the unknown. Real academic leaders promise change, and change can be painful. Change often involves learning new ways to do things, rethinking what already seems to make sense, and altering your firmly held world view. No wonder some people are more comfortable choosing the second-best candidate.

I don't mean to suggest that those who do choose to remain in a position for a long tenure are necessarily paper shufflers. Countless deans and presidents have served long tenures during which they did much to distinguish their institutions. They deserve our respect and admiration.

And I don't mean to suggest that there are no administrators who place their careers first and who care little about the institution they are supposedly serving.

But the existence of some selfish individuals does not justify characterizing every amibitious administrator that way, and it certainly doesn't justify choosing the second-rated candidate over the first.

The relevant question is not whether a given administrator is too ambitious or will stay in the job for a certain period of time or is just using your college to move up the ladder. The relevant question is: Are you moving forward or treading water? Is the unit growing in strength, prestige, and reputation? Are you being asked to accept change or the status quo? Are you better off now than in the recent past?

Is the candidate in question an academic leader or simply an administrator?

In the coming academic year, I will be searching for a few new department heads, and you can be certain that I'll be paying close attention to who among the candidates seems to have vaulting ambition and who doesn't. I don't believe in settling for second best.

❖   ❖   ❖

The Proper Way to Court

Winter is the season of the campus interview. Newly minted Ph.D.'s, midcareer professors, and even candidates for high-level professorial and administrative posts have, by now, survived several rounds of vetting and interviewing. The most successful have been invited as finalists to visit the campus, usually for a grueling few days of formal meetings and presentations, informal meet-and-greets, and countless meals and receptions.

Each year columnists, advisers, and career counselors weigh in with advice for the job seekers, but what about tips for the interviewers? What are the dos and don'ts for those who are organizing a campus visit?

Arguably, the most crucial stage of the recruitment process is the campus interview: When it's poorly executed, potential recruits leave with a bad impression of your institution; when it's well done, they not only walk away impressed, but people on the campus also will have had enough interaction with the candidates to make a meaningful recommendation.

Perhaps the single most-important strategy in building a strong institution is aggressive recruiting of first-rate candidates (as opposed to passive "searching"—i.e., posting an ad and waiting to see who applies). That is just as true for entry-level faculty members as it is for new deans and presidents. Investing substantial effort in the recruitment process is likely to pay considerable dividends in the future. In fact, a deftly choreographed campus visit can make the difference between losing your top candidate to a major competitor and convincing the person that your institution is infinitely superior despite rankings that might suggest otherwise.

Effective recruiting takes a considerable amount of thought and planning. The first step is to help the committee members and others involved in the search understand that the process requires wooing recruits. A natural impulse among some committee members is to play the role of grand inquisitor and to grill candidates as if they were defendants in a criminal trial. Certainly, you want to arrive at an accurate assessment of a candidate's capabilities, so a certain amount of rigorous questioning is warranted. But some people go on the attack, often embarrassing not only the candidate but other committee members as well.

Everyone involved in the process needs to understand that the campus visit is a two-way vetting process: While the institution is attempting to determine which finalist is the best fit, the candidate is similarly sizing up the campus to see if it would be a supportive and comfortable intellectual home. By the time an institution narrows a candidate pool to three or four finalists, any one of them is likely to perform well in the job. And many of them may have other interviews lined up as well. A wise committee will work diligently to treat the candidates so well that they return home impressed with the quality of the institution and feeling that they were given the red-carpet treatment.

A provost at a large research university told me that before accepting his current post he had been a candidate at another institution, where he had experienced a "dreadful" campus visit.

"I was under consideration to become the second-in-command of the university, but they treated me as if I were an entry-level worker of some kind," he said. "They had me find my own way from the airport to the hotel, failed to arrange a dinner with committee members the first night, neglected to send me an updated agenda, and on several occasions had forgotten to arrange for escorts from one meeting to the next." He couldn't help but conclude that the university was not serious about his candidacy, and he withdrew.

The objective of any search is to give candidates wide exposure to people on your campus, in formal and informal settings.

In a faculty search, that typically means plenty of opportunities for everyone in the department, including staff members, to meet with the candidate, as well as arranging for the obligatory meeting with the dean or associate dean. Some committees also schedule sessions with people outside of the department with whom the new faculty member would likely interact—the director of the teaching center, the head of the honors program, the graduate dean, or key faculty members in a discipline relevant to the candidate's research or teaching interests. The list would vary according to institutional context.

In an administrative search, the circle would be proportionately larger. Department-head candidates would need to meet with their college's council of chairs and various college officials, and they would likely have entrance and exit interviews with the dean. Vice-presidential and presidential candidates would need campuswide exposure as well as to meet key university trustees and local leaders. In a multi-campus university, candidates for positions in central administration should visit each branch campus.

Innovative search committees have devised a number of simple practices to court candidates and enhance the campus visit. Some of the ones I will list here might be reserved for high-level searches, but they are all approaches that work:

- A carefully crafted agenda is a must. Establish the schedule well in advance so that committee members and others can reserve specific dates and times on their busy schedules. Some committees set the date of the campus visit at the very beginning of the search process, months before the actual interview.

- Provide a little free time for the candidates periodically throughout the schedule, but especially right before they have to give a public presentation. That allows them time to freshen up, collect their thoughts, and so on.

- Provide each candidate with a detailed agenda and a list of committee members in advance of the visit.

- Arrange for someone to greet each candidate at the airport and provide transportation to the hotel.

- Choose a decent hotel, not the least expensive or the one closest to the campus with lumpy beds. Some committees put the candidate up in the most interesting places available locally—a charming bed-and-breakfast, for example or, in the case of institutions in especially desirable locations, seaside resorts, casino hotels, or establishments in historic districts. Remember: The objective here is to impress.

- Take the extra step of arranging for the candidate to receive a gift basket at check-in time. Typically it would include fruit, nuts, snacks, bottled water, and gifts containing the university logo—coffee mugs and the like.

- For administrative searches, provide a stipend to pay two or three student ambassadors to usher candidates from meeting to meeting and to provide a campus tour.

- For meals, choose restaurants that will leave a good impression, especially those that might be unique to the culture of the community. (And always inquire in advance if the candidate has dietary restrictions; you wouldn't want to take someone with fish allergies to the local seafood bistro or sushi bar.)

- Assemble a packet of brochures, booklets, and magazines that showcase university programs and community attractions. They help candidates imagine themselves as part of the community.

- Arrange for the candidate to spend time with a realtor to tour neighborhoods.

There is no "correct" set of procedures for running an ideal search. Each committee will need to make choices given the institution's unique circumstances. The key point here is that the committee that makes a conscious effort to recruit—that is, to actively woo—candidates during the campus visit stands the best chance to win over its top choice.

❖   ❖   ❖

But She Was Our Top Choice

Some years ago a young colleague rushed into my office and slammed the desk with the flat of his hand. He had been serving on the search committee for a new university president and had just learned that the Board of Trustees—the legal hiring authority—had chosen not the committee's favorite candidate but one of the two other finalists the committee had deemed "acceptable."

"I am outraged," he blustered. "The committee was clear that we almost unanimously supported the other candidate as our top choice, but the trustees simply disregarded the faculty's voice." He characterized the process as "corrupt" and as a flagrant example of the erosion of shared governance.

I have heard that identical sentiment expressed about almost every conceivable type of academic search. But the sentiment is based on the mistaken belief that a committee—or an entire department or college—selects (in effect, "elects" by popular vote) a new hire.

In academe the almost universal tradition is for search committees to forward an unranked list of acceptable candidates to whomever has the authority to make a final decision. That tradition is far from corrupt or undemocratic.

The problem is that things get complicated in practice. Often the board or the administrator who will make the final hire will formally request an unranked list, but is informally interested in knowing who the committee thinks is the top candidate. (That was the case with my young colleague above.) At other times the search committee will rank the candidates even if it is has not been asked to.

I would argue that asking a committee to provide an unranked list of the top finalists is both an example of shared governance at its best and the practice that makes the most sense.

Shared governance, especially in the context of a search for a top administrator, means that professors, staff members, and sometimes students get to participate in the process—unlike the bad old days when a university official could hire whomever he (and it was invariably a male) wanted without any input. "Shared" means that everyone has a role:

- The search committee evaluates applications, selects a short-list of candidates, conducts preliminary interviews, contacts references, chooses a group of finalists to invite to campus, solicits input about the candidates from appropriate stakeholders, and determines which of the finalists are acceptable.

- Then it's up to the final decision maker, who is responsible for conducting background checks and entering into formal negotiations with the front-runner.

"Shared" doesn't mean that every constituency gets to participate at every stage.

Someone has to exercise "due diligence" and contact the front-runner's present and former superiors to discover if there are any known skeletons that are likely to re-emerge. I have seen due diligence prevent some disastrous hires: the candidate for a deanship who had concealed the fact that he had recently been fired; the vice-presidential candidate who had embezzled funds; the prospective chairman who had been disciplined for sexual misconduct.

Clearly, the main reason why a search—especially for an administrator—cannot be a simple matter of a popular vote is that someone must remain accountable for the final decision, and committees cannot be held accountable.

I see at least three compelling reasons why a search committee would be asked to present a list of unranked candidates.

First, if, as a dean, I am conducting background checks and discover a problem serious enough to prevent me from pursuing a candidate further, then I can unobtrusively move on to the next candidate on the list without revealing the problem to anyone. That seems appropriate, given that such problems usually involve confidential personnel matters.

Second, if I do eliminate a candidate, or if I negotiate with a candidate and fail to come to terms, I certainly don't want everyone to know that the individual we finally do hire was the second, or even third, choice. I know of one search for a department head that resulted in the hiring of the sixth-ranked candidate. She had to suffer a great deal of humiliation at the hands of thoughtless colleagues who made it clear to her that they were well aware of her ranking. No one should be put at such a disadvantage.

Finally, and most important, if I am the person in charge of making the final hire, I should have the opportunity to choose the candidate in whom I have the most confidence, and often that is a matter of personal chemistry. A president presented with three acceptable finalists for the position of provost should have the latitude to choose the one he or she feels most comfortable with, since the two of them will work very closely.

The same applies to other administrative positions. If you are hiring someone who is to report directly to you, surely you would want to select the finalist in whom you have the most trust and confidence.

Even searches for tenure-track faculty members should follow a similar pattern, although it is true that many departments tend to treat the selection of new colleagues as a simple vote. While the consequences of hiring a tainted provost are potentially much graver than those of hiring a tainted assistant professor, the same principles apply.

I know of a search in which a vigilant department chairman discovered that the new Ph.D. he was about to make an offer to had recently been charged with sexual harassment for coercing an undergraduate into a relationship. The chairman wisely chose to cancel the search.

I don't mean to suggest that all academic searches will conform to the principles of shared governance, or that all individuals in charge of searches will have purely unselfish motives, or that all participants in searches will competently fulfill their respective roles in the process.

An institution's formal policies regarding searches may well trump some of the principles I have outlined here. All I am suggesting is that in order to conduct genuinely effective searches, all parties need a clear understanding of one another's roles in the process. Perhaps then, distrust and hurt feelings—not to mention a few bruised hands—might be avoided.

The Academic Job Search and the Internet

Last week three executive-search consultants—headhunters, as they are called—scheduled telephone interviews with me to conduct reference checks on candidates for senior administrative positions. I'm a reference for the candidates, all of whom have advanced to the stage of finalist, and the headhunters were "exercising due diligence" by investigating whether the candidates would be a good fit for the institution the consultants represented.

One of the consultants spent an unusually long time in the interview tiptoeing around what clearly was his real concern: whether the candidate had any skeletons in the closet that would come back to haunt the university.

After gently but somewhat awkwardly inquiring about whether there were any "controversies" that he should be aware of, the consultant finally blurted out: "Look, it's a lot different nowadays from when you and I came up through the ranks. In the old days there was no Internet. Today, anyone can Google a candidate and gather a whole range of information, but who knows how reliable or accurate the information is?"

Another headhunter told me that the real problem was that various constituents use information they glean from the Internet to further their own political objectives—even going so far as to sabotage the candidacy of one finalist because they favor another. "It's very frustrating," she said. "We are constantly doing damage control because committee members or even just other faculty on campus will dredge up what they believe to be damning information on one candidate or another."

Occasionally, she added, an entire search is aborted because of someone's Internet sleuthing. "People who engage in this kind of amateur detective work really end up shooting themselves in the foot," she said. "They do incredible damage to the institution. If they truly want to be helpful, they need to let the process take its course."

Of course, sometimes information obtained from a Web search can help prevent an institution from making a serious mistake. On a number of occasions, search committees at institutions where I have worked averted disaster by discovering via the Internet a potential problem with a candidate and then independently confirming the information.

In one instance, a department chair who was conducting a search for a junior faculty member discovered a news story revealing that the top candidate had been fired for sexual misconduct. After verifying that the information was true, the chair terminated the finalist's candidacy.

In another case, a candidate for a deanship had presented himself as a sitting dean at his home institution when, in fact, he had been forced to resign from that post six months earlier. Misrepresenting your credentials is a serious transgression, and that candidate, too, was eliminated from the pool once the facts had been verified.

Too bad it is often so difficult to separate fact from fiction on the Web. Just because it's been published doesn't make it true, even in a newspaper article. Exercising genuine due diligence on a candidate's background means thoroughly investigating information that seems disturbing or suspicious rather than simply trusting the source and assuming its validity. A thorough vetting may require numerous phone calls to parties in the know, but serious follow-through is essential to preserve the integrity of the search.

Most executive-search consultants are experts at the vetting process because their companies' reputations are at stake. They will contact several people who are not listed as references on the candidate's application—present and former supervisors, and even officials at previous institutions where the candidate once worked. They will also commission professional background investigations, which include verifying the candidate's earned academic degrees as well as conducting a complete credit history and a criminal-background check.

Proper due diligence also means carefully assessing the information obtained from conversations with "off list" references. A reference may be very negative about a candidate, but there may be a reason—the candidate and reference may have a longstanding personality conflict, or the two may have become professional rivals. Search committees and consultants must sort through the various narratives and determine, as much as is possible, the truth.

Some years ago during a search that I conducted for a leadership position, I spoke with the candidate's former dean, who proceeded to excoriate the candidate. The picture the dean painted was highly unflattering. Rather than accept his narrative at face value, I spoke with the provost at the same institution. She immediately made clear that the former dean had a vendetta against our candidate because of a bitter power struggle that had occurred some years before. I ended up hiring the candidate, with no regrets.

Vetting a candidate is a tricky business, and that's why search committees should resist allowing people from outside the committee to contaminate a search by producing damning information from the Internet. The responsibility for due diligence always lies with the committee—and with the search firm if one has been hired.

The Internet has affected academic recruiting in other ways, especially searches for senior administrators. In the days before the Web, an institution conducting a search for a new president, say, could quietly woo an official from a rival campus without anyone the wiser until very late in the process. Today, however, the names of finalists—and, often, even semifinalists—are posted on the Web and their candidacies instantaneously outed at their home institutions.

This development is good for openness, but it also has a downside: It can discourage some potentially excellent candidates from applying for fear of embarrassing their home institutions. Just last week, a vice president at an institution in the East called to ask my advice. She is being courted by a search firm for a college presidency and is interested in the job, but "terrified" that her president will "take it personally" that she is considering leaving. "I just don't know how to negotiate exploring the position without burning bridges here," she lamented.

In fact, she may not even have to rely on her president's casually picking the news up from the Internet. I know of several instances where the local newspapers have the names of university officials on Google Alert, which notifies you whenever a particular name appears online. By using that application, the hometown newspaper can potentially be the first to break the story locally when a university official becomes a candidate at another institution.

Needless to say, the Web has also had a positive effect on recruiting. Because so much information about an institution is now available on its Web site (and on other sites as well), candidates have much more opportunity to become thoroughly knowledgeable about the place. And candidates do seem to be better prepared for interviews than in the pre-Internet days—and we now expect them to be. In that way, the Internet has helped raise the bar in the search process.

In addition, more and more colleges are using the Internet to help them conduct first-rate searches.

Some committees construct elaborate Web sites devoted to the search. The site might include the names and short bios of committee members, an expanded version of the position description, the vitae and other materials of finalists, helpful institutional links that guide applicants to especially relevant Web pages within the university (strategic plan, master plan, budget, and so on), and external links to important or impressive attractions within the community or region. In that way, the Internet has become an invaluable recruiting tool.

When it comes to academic recruiting, the Internet itself is neutral; it is how we use it that potentially can be useful or destructive to the process. If we use it as a constructive tool, our searches become all the more effective and efficient. If we use it as a weapon, we potentially hurt ourselves, our candidates, and our institutions.

❖   ❖   ❖

I'm Your Millstone

A dean I know is a staunch advocate of reform in how universities treat spousal hires, especially for senior positions. Her own experience convinced her that academe is far too inflexible about dual-career hires and that, as a result, many institutions inadvertently work against their own best interests.

Before assuming her current position, she had been named a finalist for a deanship at another institution. She had been especially excited about the job because the university was fairly prestigious and sponsored one of the nation's premier doctoral programs in her field. A prominent scholar, she would have brought additional prestige to an already first-rate program.

Her campus interview had gone exceedingly well, and all indications were that she would be offered the position. To her surprise and chagrin, the head of the search committee called one Saturday afternoon to say that, despite her successful campus visit, she would not receive an offer. She didn't get the nod, the committee chair intimated, because the university would have had to bear the added expense of hiring her spouse—a noted scholar in his own right.

The couple was understandably disappointed. She told me that over dinner that same evening her husband had said ruefully, "I'm very sorry, dear, but I'm afraid I've become your millstone."

The irony is that the dean's husband was not truly a "trailing" spouse if by that term we mean an unequal partner—someone who, in the worst-case scenarios, is being dragged along like a dead weight. Indeed, he would have been every bit as much of a catch for the institution as the dean. It would have been a rare win-win situation.

Unfortunately for all concerned, the powers-that-be did not recognize the opportunity.

All too often we as administrators fail to make the important distinction between partners who most likely would not have been hired under normal circumstances and, thus, could be a burden on an institution, and those who would be an attractive hire under any circumstances. One is a "trailing" spouse in need of "an accommodation"; the other, for lack of a more elegant phrase, is an integral part of a recruitment package.

An institution takes on a trailing spouse (or partner) with a sense of obligation—as part of the price it has to pay for the individual it really wants. And sometimes it does so with resentment. In contrast, a university takes on (or should) a package of two high-performing professionals with enthusiasm and pride.

That is precisely the kind of language that higher-education publications tend to use in reporting on an institution's "great coup" in attracting a "dynamic duo" from a rival institution. One department is said to have "snatched" two stars from the other, or to have "lured" the couple away. The recipient institution gets credit for wise strategic recruitment while the other is implicitly blamed for its failure to retain the couple.

Clearly, hiring the superstar partner of a superstar is substantially different from negotiating a job offer for someone who could legitimately be called a trailing spouse. The key distinction that should always be at the forefront of such decisions is whether hiring someone's partner genuinely enhances and contributes to the department and its programs in appreciable ways.

Perhaps some departments fall into the trap of automatically classifying all spousal hires as undesirable, out of fear of ending up with an unacceptable or mediocre colleague. We all know of situations in which a university official exerted pressure on a department to accept a spouse or partner that the department felt was not a good fit. No department likes to feel that a colleague was foisted on it, and such situations have left a bad taste in the mouth of many a faculty member regarding spousal hires.

It would be a real mistake, however, to assume that just because some dual-career hires have gone bad (usually because of a lack of faculty participation in the process), all such hires are to be avoided. In effect, some departments have allowed the legitimate concern about undue pressure to blind them to the obvious benefits that could accrue to a department that actively sets out to recruit a high-achieving couple.

That is the case with the dean and her so-called millstone husband: Both are popular and well-respected members of their current institution. Some of the best hires I have made over the years have been dual-career couples who ended up contributing substantially to a department's culture and prestige. In fact, in a few cases, colleagues have commented that the partner was "even more of a catch" or "even more impressive" than the principal hire.

Of course, the effort to appoint a partner needs to be handled with deftness and sensitivity. Above all, the process needs to be open and transparent. While the search may not be as elaborate as a traditional one, the affected department must be afforded the opportunity to vet the candidate's credentials thoroughly.

The department should also have the opportunity to invite the candidate to a campus visit, although in some cases, the candidate may be so well-known that a department will dispense with that ritual. The advantage of a visit is that it helps both the new recruit and the department feel that the process has integrity and legitimacy. The principal objection to the good-old-boy scenario of an administrator pressuring a department to accept a partner is that its faculty members feel voiceless, that their input was neither solicited nor desired.

In determining the trailing spouse's starting salary, the administrator who makes the offer should be cognizant of salary compression and inversion issues with existing faculty members in the department. Many academics are suspicious of the whole notion of spousal hiring in general, so there is no need to add to the tensions by introducing inequities from the start.

Finally, once the partner joins the faculty, the department must treat him or her as a full member of the departmental community, not as an interloper. Some departments have made the serious mistake of treating a spouse or partner not as a fellow colleague but as the "chair's wife" or the "dean's partner" or the institution's "first lady." If recruiting a dynamic package of two high-performing professionals is going to work, then both partners must be accepted as individuals.

My point is that the real millstone is not someone's partner; it is the debilitating fear that a spousal hire will necessarily disadvantage the department. My experience is that it usually is the reverse: A carefully vetted spousal hire can add immeasurably to a department and an institution.

6

Special Topics

♦

Commencement Matters

A few weeks ago, some colleagues and I were sharing stories about graduation ceremonies, and the discussion reminded me of at least two very
different ways of thinking about the role of commencement in the contemporary university.

Should it be viewed primarily as an academic ritual or as a celebration?

The first view was articulated recently by a fellow provost, who is
just retiring after a long and distinguished career. He shook his head sadly
and said, "Graduation is not what it used to be. It's lost its seriousness,
its gravitas."

A business dean, who is much earlier in his career, disagreed. "I kind
of like the festiveness that we see these days," he replied. "Graduation used
to be too staid and pretentious. That's not my idea of a celebration."

I have to admit, early in my career, I felt exactly as my fellow provost
does. I believed that commencement was a supremely academic exercise,
the culmination of years of study and rigor, and that the ceremony should,
therefore, reflect the seriousness of that work and the achievement it symbol-
izes. I, too, was shocked by the behavior I witnessed at some ceremonies.

Of course, at the time I was on the faculty of a large research university in Florida, a state notorious for fun and sun. Thousands of students
and relatives attended our graduation ceremonies. And one never knew
what to expect.

At times, oversized beach balls would suddenly appear out of nowhere and be tossed back and forth among spectators in the large arena where we conducted the ceremony. University attendants would scramble to try to capture the projectiles.

Fraternities and sororities would orchestrate loud cheering sections to applaud each of their members as they crossed the stage. Over time, the Greek groups engaged in a fierce competition to be the loudest advocates for their own members.

As they crossed the stage, some graduates would stop midway, face the crowd, and thrust their fists skyward, while others would perform a stylized strut as if to say, "Look how cool I am." On one occasion, a graduate crossing the stage to shake hands with the university president became so carried away with emotion that instead of shaking hands he swept her into a bear hug. Unflustered and to the amazement of all, the president did not skip a beat; she recovered instantly, just in time to shake the next student's hand. (She even somehow managed not to lose her tam in the process.)

And, of course, there were the graduates who sought to subvert the pomp and ceremony of drab academic regalia by making a fashion statement. They wore flamboyant clothing that was clearly visible despite their regalia. They had colorful leis around their necks. Or they donned shorts and sandals so that onlookers might be tempted to believe that the graduate was nude under the academic robe.

Then there were the air horns, which would periodically blare out from various locations in the stands, despite the administration's best efforts to prohibit them from graduation.

At two separate ceremonies, the proceedings were briefly interrupted when streakers, wearing nothing but mortar boards, raced across the stage. (On one such occasion, a doctoral student whom I had just hooded turned to me and joked, "I told you a college education today will cost the shirt off your back—and apparently more.")

While Florida may well be known as a "fun" state, my colleagues across the country confirm that similar types of behavior are common in their own commencement exercises. Like my fellow provost, I felt for a long time that such interruptions degraded the dignity of this quintessentially academic event. But perhaps I was wrong.

It is true that university commencements are meant to applaud academic achievement, and given that only one of four people ever earns a college degree in the United States, doing so is truly a remarkable feat.

But we sometimes forget that the word "commence" means begin, not end. More than anything else, commencement is a celebration of a new phase in the graduate's life.

For some students, it marks their entry into a profession. For others it marks their eligibility to extend their education through graduate and professional schools or some other area of advanced study. For yet others, it is a new sense of self-confidence and self-respect.

It may seem like blasphemy to say so (as it would have to me decades ago), but a commencement ceremony is less an academic ritual than an advancement event. It is a big formal party.

It's about helping to make graduates proud not only of their own accomplishments but also of their institutions. It's about making the graduates' relatives feel warm and fuzzy about the campus as well. It's about formalizing the transformation from students to dedicated alumni. It's about reminding faculty members of the central role they play in shaping their students' futures. It's about reminding alumni of why they are so committed to the institution. It's about promoting the university to all its constituents—and for all the right reasons.

In short, it is about positioning people to develop relationships with the institution that will increase the likelihood that they will give back, in one way or another, to their beloved alma mater. In fact, at some universities, it's the development office, and not academic affairs or student services, that is responsible for organizing and sponsoring the commencement ceremony.

The university where I now work boasts the only college of pharmacy in the state and one of the best in the western United States. The students have a longstanding tradition of playing a prank on the dean at the annual commencement exercise. It's a well-organized ritual. During the portion of the ceremony where the pharmacy graduates cross the stage and shake hands with their dean, each one hands the dean an object that reflects the theme they have chosen for the year's prank. One year each student handed the dean a flower. Another time it was a piece of a puzzle. Members of yet another class thought of themselves as guinea pigs because they were the first to study under a drastically altered curriculum, so each student handed the dean a small bag of guinea-pig food.

Last year, as I participated in my first commencement at this university, I was momentarily taken aback as each pharmacy graduate solemnly handed the dean a potato (we are in Idaho, after all). The dean would grin sheepishly, accept it, and shake hands. As the pile of potatoes rose, an attendant slipped onto the stage with a potato sack to collect the mementos. My initial reaction was to raise my eyebrows at all the potatoes, but then I remembered: This is the students' day, not mine. Let them have their much-deserved fun. And they did.

❖   ❖   ❖

Can You Spare A Dime?

It's not uncommon to hear administrators at public universities joke that their institutions once were "state supported," then became "state assisted" and now are merely "state located."

The loss of state support has had a substantial impact on academic programs, with universities often left scrambling to fill the gap. In light of those cutbacks, the role of fund raising is ever more important to the health and development of academic programs.

Unfortunately, many academics disdain fund raising—and even, at times, the professionals employed by their institutions to do it.

A former colleague once told me that he saw fund raisers as nothing more than "oily, used-car-salesman types." His image of the development officer was of the glad-hander always poised to pounce; he couldn't see himself in the role. "If I had wanted to be a salesman," he retorted wryly, "I would have gone into selling Volvos."

A department chairwoman at the same institution complained that it was nearly impossible to interest her faculty in activities related to fund raising. "They all say that they just want to be left alone to do their teaching and research," she told me, "and they expect me to single-handedly find new donors, steward the ones we have, and bring in the additional dollars that will make their jobs easier."

Implicit in such negative characterizations is the belief that development activities somehow taint the purer activities of teaching and research, that academics who engage in fund raising are compromising their core values. In effect, the self-interested activity of fund raising is thought to erode the disinterested pursuit of knowledge.

Far from tainting the academic enterprise, however, fund raising has become an essential tool for fostering the very academic endeavors that we all so ardently cherish. Public institutions are learning (as the privates learned long ago) that now more than ever it is essential that they discover ways to reduce their reliance on state assistance.

To the extent that an institution depends too much on state support, it places in jeopardy its programs, centers, institutes, adjuncts, instructors, and summer school, because those are precisely the areas that typically are cut each time the state demands that a university accept a smaller portion of state dollars.

Fund-raising endeavors will only be successful if professors and administrators begin to recognize development officers as their allies, not as interlopers irrelevant to the academic enterprise.

Many of us work in buildings named after prominent donors. Some of us hold chaired professorships bearing the names of generous benefactors. Many of our students have received scholarships supported by private dollars. Those and other benefits were made possible by the generosity of friends of the institution.

In an age when public support of public education is dwindling, we desperately need the assistance of private donors—friends who recognize the value and centrality of academic work, friends who understand and are sympathetic to our mission, friends who are willing and able to support our work, both morally and financially. All of that has changed the job of academic leader from what it was in the past.

Effective department heads find ways to keep in touch with alumni, inviting them to campus from time to time for organized events. They also keep in touch with emeritus faculty members, another potential source of external dollars. Effective deans do all of that, too, and serve as tireless promoters of the college's programs and departments—not only to audiences within the institution but also, and more crucially, to those in the surrounding city.

But administrators can't do the job alone. The success of a fund-raising effort will depend on the participation of faculty members. The fund raisers—the department chair, dean, president, or development officer—must know what to promote to donors and how to promote it, but only faculty members can craft the story that will inspire the donor's support.

As a dean overseeing 16 academic departments and several institutes, centers, and other worthy entities, I need to know before I visit with potential donors which priorities a department wishes to champion and precisely why they are worthy of support:

- Does the physics department want me to secure money to up-grade our planetarium, or would it rather increase the budget of its Intense Laser Physics Institute?

- Would the anthropology department prefer that I concentrate on finding support for its field archaeology program, or for its Centre for the Study of Rural Ireland—or both?

- Does the School of Communication wish to obtain additional support for the student television station or for its nationally prominent forensics team?

If I am to assist a department in realizing its goals, I need to know which priorities to concentrate on and exactly what it is about a given project that will inspire and excite. Why should a donor be encouraged to invest in it? Only faculty and staff members intimately involved in the project—and then the department as a whole when it identifies its priori-ties—can best position the dean, the president, and the professional fund raisers to articulate the department's needs and to excite donors about the project.

Without the help of those who are intimately involved, we lack the specificity to be persuasive.

Fund raising, then, is a team effort, but despite the fears of some faculty members, no one is asking them to become fund raisers; we employ professionals to do that job. What I am saying is that if our academic programs and projects are going to be competitive in the face of decreased public support, then we must engage in strategic fund raising; and if our development efforts are going to be successful, then they necessarily require the participation of professors, who along with students are the heart and soul of the academic enterprise.

It wasn't many years ago when those of us who identify strongly as scholars or intellectuals would disparage fund raising as an activity that sullied the life of the mind. Development was seen as a crass activity that no self-respecting scholar should ever stoop to. But now we live in a very different era and work in a very different academy. We can no longer afford those prejudices.

Far from being someone to avoid, the fund raiser is the academic's new best friend and ally.

❖ ❖ ❖

The Ethics of Technology

A senior professor recently asked permission to post an announcement promoting an antiwar rally on our college's official e-mail announcement list. Although the rally was to take place on the campus, it was not a university-sponsored event.

When I explained that it would be inappropriate, and indeed unethical, to use the college's official communication medium to announce events unrelated to the conduct of official college business, he seemed shocked and replied, "Surely, everyone in the college is against the war." I pointed out that regardless of an event's worthiness, university resources may not be used for personal communication.

In a similar case, I know of a department chairman at a public university who was reprimanded for using his office computer and university e-mail account to engage in day trading on the stock market. He closely monitored stock fluctuations throughout the day, constantly buying and selling shares. He had even bragged to colleagues that he was "raking in the dough."

That chairman was genuinely stunned when his behavior came under the scrutiny of university auditors and he was judged guilty of misusing state property and engaging in personal activities during work hours—clear conflicts of interest for which he nearly lost his job.

Those cases are representative of what turns out to be widespread misunderstanding about the appropriate use of university technology.

Many professors, staff members, and even administrators see campus computers and e-mail accounts as their own private property—a type of employment benefit provided with no constraints on use. The fact is, universities "assign" computer equipment to us as tools to help us perform our jobs more effectively and efficiently, in the same way that institutions assign offices to faculty members, laboratory space to scientists, or photocopy machines to departments. Computer equipment, far from being personal property, is owned and maintained by the university, with restrictions on how it may be used.

Broader ethical principles are at play as well. For example, while it is generally considered unethical to use university e-mail accounts to engage in personal communication, most institutions are tolerant when it comes to minor personal usage, such as inviting friends to lunch or cocktails.

But institutions frown on extensive personal use, such as carrying on lengthy private exchanges or selling personal property on eBay, not to mention engaging in day trading or political advocacy. Those are all abuses to one degree or another.

A university chief information officer explains it by using an analogy: "It's the equivalent of petty theft at the supermarket, where we each have our own personal threshold as to what is morally acceptable." Some of us think nothing of popping a few grapes in our mouths while in the produce section, he explained, while others justify keeping an extra $20 bill that the cashier mistakenly gave in making change.

"Regardless of where you draw the line," he said, "it is all theft, pure and simple."

That sentiment is echoed in my own state. Illinois mandates that all state employees—including faculty and staff members, and student workers at all public universities—take an annual online ethics course. It presents principles relevant to ethical workplace behavior, illustrates them in narra- tive scenarios, and then quizzes the test takers. Prominent in that training are discussions on the use of state-provided technology for personal use.

Many professors and administrators avoid even the appearance of impropriety by establishing external e-mail accounts for personal use. That allows them to draw clear boundaries between university business and personal or recreational use.

"I have a free Hotmail account for all my nonuniversity e-mailing," said one professor of zoology. "I only use my university account for communicating with students and colleagues in the discipline."

Maintaining a personal account not only helps you avoid ethical transgressions, it also can protect you from unexpected legal trouble. A common legal tactic nowadays is to obtain someone's e-mail messages through a public-information request. Those messages can be easy to obtain because public universities often archive e-mail traffic for a given amount of time.

You may have thought the messages you deleted yesterday were gone forever, but they could still be retrievable. The university is allowed to archive employee e-mail messages because it, in effect, owns them: They were produced in a university-provided e-mail account by a university employee, most likely using a university-owned computer.

I know of one faculty member who was sued for libel by a colleague. He was shocked and embarrassed when a public-information request turned up a number of incriminating messages. He might have avoided being exposed had he only used a personal account.

The same ethical principles pertain to an institution's e-mail discussion list. The professor who wanted to post an antiwar announcement claimed that the e-mail list was a "virtual faculty lounge" and so he should be permitted the same kind of free speech as in an actual faculty lounge.

While it is a type of public space, a college discussion list is necessarily a restricted space and, like e-mail accounts, is primarily a tool to assist in the performance of one's job. While most universities are somewhat flexible with actual usage in the same way that they are with e-mail, the identical ethical principles apply.

What's more, supervisors would be wise to exercise oversight over the content of their official e-mail discussion lists because, unlike e-mail, the supervisors are directly accountable for what gets posted. That is why every official discussion group should have a single moderator who can make informed judgments about which messages are appropriate to post.

Another common misconception about the ethical use of university technology involves computer software. Most universities purchase site licenses that give them the legal right to provide certain software programs to a specified number of users. Usually, those software programs are the only ones that are supposed to be installed on university computers. That helps the university protect itself from legal liability, and it also helps to cut down on the number of software applications that conflict with university software, thereby causing system errors.

Nonetheless, many faculty members attempt to install their own software on machines assigned to them, arguing that they will use the software primarily to conduct official business.

Campus information-technology departments don't see it that way. They are charged with serving the tech needs of faculty and staff members, but they are also obligated to report infractions by those users. That conflict often creates an unnecessarily adversarial relationship between the two.

That relationship is also strained when professors ask a technology-support staff member to work on, or repair, their personal computers—another ethical no-no. The professors' rationale is that they are using the home computer or laptop principally for official business.

But technology staff members are employed to work on equipment owned by the institution. Asking them to work on your home computer creates a conflict of interest. In the case of a public university, it would amount to using taxpayer money to service private property. An obvious solution to that dilemma is for you to employ the technician outside of the university setting as an independent contractor. Even better: Hire someone unconnected to the university.

Practices and policies vary by institution, and private colleges have much more leeway than public ones in determining what is permissible. My point here is that too often we take our university-provided technology for granted and assume we have much more latitude than we do. It is our responsibility both to know the ethical principles at stake and the institutional rules pertaining to technology use—which, after all, are in place for the greater good.

❖ ❖ ❖

E-mails Are Forever

A noted scholar contacted me last month and asked me to write a column about e-mail etiquette. She was troubled by the "lack of respect" and "sometimes outright hostility" that some of her colleagues routinely conveyed in messages. E-mail, she said, seems to "give folks license to be rude and downright nasty."

Coincidentally, a department chairman had written with a similar request a few weeks earlier. He had found himself embroiled in a departmental squabble after offending some of his colleagues with an e-mail message in which he unintentionally sounded imperious and bossy. "I was simply trying to explain a new university policy," he said. "I didn't mean to sound like a dictator."

E-mail has been around long enough that you'd think we would have learned how to handle it by now. But I've heard plenty of similar complaints lately from other victims of e-mail hostility or misunderstanding. At professional conferences, deans and other administrators spend an increasing amount of time discussing the topic of problematic e-mail practices. By all accounts, the problem is only getting worse.

Administrators and faculty members use e-mail in a number of inappropriate ways. Some employ the "cc" function as a weapon. A faculty member becomes angry with a colleague and complains to that colleague in an e-mail message, but rather than resolve the matter privately, the sender will "cc" the recipient's supervisor and perhaps even the supervisor's supervisor. A private exchange that might have generated mutual understanding instead draws management into the dispute.

Some academics have made a habit of firing off angry e-mail messages to a host of recipients. I know an engineering professor who periodically becomes frustrated by some new university policy and responds by sending a heated e-mail message to the university's president, selected trustees, the provost, his dean, and every faculty member in his large department, excoriating "the university" for adopting the policy in question.

Dispatching a message to such a broad group of recipients is not only a breach of protocol (which dictates that you typically communicate to the next level above you), but it is invariably counterproductive: Your objective was to encourage people to take action, but the likely result is that you have succeeded in casting yourself as a crank or a troublemaker—someone not to be taken seriously.

Other academics are utterly abusive in e-mail messages. It is difficult to imagine the senders uttering the same incendiary words in a face-to-face encounter. I've seen colleagues use e-mail to accuse each other of stealing research ideas, of being "stupid" and therefore not deserving of their doctorate, of being "a disgrace to the professoriate," and of "destroying the department." A colleague of mine refers to such unrestrained verbal onslaughts as "assault by e-mail."

The most generous explanations for that behavior are that the sender fired off the message in the heat of anger or was simply unaware of how insulting it would sound. Regardless of the rationalization, there is no excuse for abusive language in the workplace—none.

That said, it is true that you have little control over how recipients perceive the tone of your message, even a routine one.

A senior scholar in the humanities said she was puzzled when some of her doctoral students would send messages asking if she was angry or upset with them. "It took me a while to realize that they were responding to the pithiness of my own e-mails," she explained. "I use e-mail as infrequently as possible and only to transact business, so I am not chatty or especially warm." Her students confused brevity with disapproval—a perception that was undoubtedly magnified by the anxiety that dissertators experience. She began to make a special effort to make her messages less chilly.

Some people make the mistake of committing sensitive information to an e-mail message, forgetting that, once composed, it becomes a permanent record that can be shared with anyone and everyone. I know of a professor serving on a tenure committee who made the mistake of explaining to his colleague in an e-mail message why the committee had voted against her tenure. Obviously, it is unethical to discuss such personnel issues outside of the committee to begin with, but by revealing the decision-making process in writing, he inadvertently gave his colleague and her lawyer a document that later became the centerpiece of a successful lawsuit.

Here are some best practices to help faculty members and administrators avoid such unhappy situations:

Be judicious in deciding who should receive your message. Before adding any names to the "cc" list, ask yourself, Will adding someone to the list embarrass the main recipient or cause other difficulties? Am I sending the message only to those who need to read it? What is my real purpose here, and can I better achieve it in person, or on the phone? As a general rule, refrain from sending messages to a long list of recipients.

Consider the tone of your messages. Do you inadvertently sound condescending, angry, bullying, or inappropriate in any way?

People reading a message are not always able to "hear" tonal subtleties, so it is best to avoid sarcasm, irony, and satire in workplace e-mail messages. Similarly, using all uppercase may come across as shouting. Long-winded, rambling messages may sound argumentative, whiny, or even bad-tempered, while brief ones may seem cold and unfriendly. Avoid either extreme.

Resist the urge to fight fire with fire. The best response to a heated or insulting message is not to reply immediately. Good practice dictates that you take some time to cool off and reflect about how to answer. Some experts suggest that you compose a reply but then save it and reread it later. See if you feel the same way. Above all, never send important e-mail messages when you are tired, angry, or upset—or late at night when you might be all three.

When you do reply to a negative message, avoid being drawn into a lengthy back-and-forth exchange that may only serve to escalate the conflict. Attempt to resolve the difficulty in person: "It appears that we are talking at cross-purposes; let's meet tomorrow and work this out."

Compose every e-mail message as if the entire world will read it. While you may well be engaging in a "private" exchange with a colleague or supervisor, e-mail is by definition a public forum. Be cautious and thoughtful about what you commit to writing and how you phrase your messages. If an issue is especially delicate or controversial, pick up the phone.

Above all, in workplace e-mail messages, be professional. Developing a professional ethos demands constant self-scrutiny. After writing the previous paragraph, I took a break to respond to a colleague's e-mail message requesting a document that I had already sent him. In resending the document, I unthinkingly reminded him that I had already sent it—a reminder that served no other purpose than to embarrass the recipient and make me feel petty.

I was quick to apologize. What you're going for here is a tone that is businesslike but warm, succinct but not telegraphic, and respectful rather than even subtly reproachful.

From time to time I receive a message saying something like, "John Doe hereby retracts the e-mail message recently sent to you." But you can never retrieve a message. That is precisely why observing the best practices of e-mail etiquette from the outset is so important. You can avoid a lot of regret by remembering a simple truth: E-mails are forever.

❖ ❖ ❖

Keep Your Emeriti Close

An education dean asked my advice recently about how to "handle" retired professors. I was astonished to learn that she, and apparently some of the department heads at her institution, viewed emeritus faculty members as a nuisance.

"They're like the proverbial bad penny," she told me. "They keep coming back around, and they interfere in departmental business as if they still worked here full time."

She assumed that, since I am a dean, I would share her view, and she hoped I had some remedy. When I explained that my college makes a special effort to embrace our emeritus faculty members and to involve them in the life of the college, she was incredulous.

Former faculty members are a storehouse of historical and procedural knowledge about their departments, colleges, and universities; they often remain active in their disciplines after retirement; many are eager to continue participating in the life of the university; and they often give back to the institution in substantive ways. An institution impoverishes itself when it fails to tap into that wealth of experience.

In fact, keeping your retired professors close can have substantial payoffs. (While some institutions reserve the title of emeritus for a distinguished subset of retirees, other universities, such as my own, use the term to refer to all retired faculty members.)

Many academic departments find ways to accommodate their retirees—by extending departmental mail privileges, setting aside a shared office on the campus, asking them to deliver public lectures or speak to student groups. Many science departments allow active researchers to maintain their laboratories and continue their work well into retirement.

Some colleges publish a regular newsletter for retirees focusing on their recent accomplishments (I like to joke that our retired professors seem more productive than our regular faculty members, but, in some cases, that's not far from the truth).

One department chairman I know has been especially successful in making retired faculty members feel like they still belong to the department. He invites them to all departmental events, often asking them to serve as guest speakers. Each year he holds a picnic at his home for former faculty members. The provost and dean typically attend as well—a nice way of showing that the top leaders haven't forgotten those faculty members. The event allows retirees to reconnect with one another and the institution.

When a faculty member is about to retire, that same chairman organizes a daylong conference in the retiree's honor. Scholars from the department and from across the country present papers and posters on subjects related to the retiree's area of research. The chairman himself takes photographs throughout the day and assembles an album for the honoree that includes both the photos and texts of the papers. What a fitting tribute to a scholar at the end of a long academic career.

That chairman's efforts have paid off in significant ways for his department. It enjoys an unusually strong sense of community across generations, and many of its emeritus professors have made substantial donations to the department to support student scholarships and a lecture series. Others have given back to the institution by offering to teach courses without compensation.

One way to recognize outstanding emeritus professors and involve them productively in the department or college is to create an emeritus-faculty advisory board.

Four years ago, my college created a board composed of 28 former faculty members that was intended to enhance the relationship between the college and its retirees for the benefit of both. The board "provides the dean with input on current college initiatives; helps narrate the institutional history of the university, particularly the history of the college; and assists in the development of new initiatives for enhancing the retirement experiences of all emeriti faculty."

The board is far from simply a feel-good social group. Its members have led important programs and served as stalwart advocates for their fellow retirees. For example, using college money, the board created a grant program to help pay for students' attendance at professional conferences. In its role as advocate, the board urged the college to intercede on behalf of retirees to persuade the library administration to grant full faculty privileges to emeritus professors rather than, as had been the case, the equivalent of student privileges. The policy was changed.

Because the board members are actively involved in the life of the college, their dedication to the university runs deep. Many board members have made financial donations to the college, including in one case a sizable estate gift.

Institutions can involve emeritus professors in a number of other ways. Each year my college considers retired faculty members for potential induction into our Hall of Fame—an honorary society composed mostly of distinguished alumni.

When I recently informed a retiree that she would be inducted into our college's Hall of Fame, she became teary-eyed and said, "I was among the first women admitted to the professoriate, and every day was a struggle for me and for other women like me around the country. Now, after all those decades, I feel validated, appreciated."

Her commitment to the institution is solid but tempered by a history of lack of recognition. Inducting her into the Hall of Fame crystallized her commitment by helping her realize that despite the challenges she faced as a woman in a male-dominated academic world, the institution values her and her many contributions to its intellectual life.

Every year my college sponsors a luncheon for retired faculty members at which the guests hear updates about the college and have the opportunity to socialize. It typically draws about 200 people and is among the most popular events we sponsor.

Certainly, the dean who asked for advice on "handling" her retired faculty members had a point: Some professors do interfere in departmental business long after they retire, attempting to exercise control over policies and practices in which they no longer have a stake. As a dean, you need to deal with those folks on an individual basis.

But in my experience, the vast majority of emeritus professors genuinely wish to remain involved in appropriate and productive ways. I, for one, intend to keep them close.

❖　❖　❖

What Deans Expect of
Department Heads

Recently I served on a panel of deans who were asked to discuss our expectations of department chairs. The session was meant to help new chairs understand their role as academic administrators. The panelists exhibited a surprising amount of unanimity on the subject, and I would like to share some of their advice.

It's become a cliché in higher-education literature to assert that the toughest job in the institution is department head, and for good reason: As chair, you have a foot in two very different worlds.

You are the chief advocate for your faculty both to the administration and externally. In that role, you are a kind of prime minister—the first among equals—and a stalwart champion of your department's interests.

Within the department, however, you are the frontline administrator, the supervisor of all personnel, and the primary fiscal agent. In that role, you serve as the chief representative of the institution to your faculty and staff members.

A key to becoming an effective department head is the ability to balance those two very different roles. Ineffective chairs foster an us-versus-them climate within the department: "You'll never guess what they are going to make us do now," such chairs say, where "they" means all university administrators above the department level lumped into one. Adopting that stance may ingratiate you to department members in the short term, but it also demonstrates a lack of leadership.

Effective chairs understand that as part of the institution's administrative team, they will be expected to interpret and even "sell" new initiatives, policies, or procedures to their departments on behalf of the institution. Leadership involves stepping up and accepting that role, even when you personally do not support the new policy.

As someone with a foot in two worlds, you will need to follow proper protocol scrupulously and guide your faculty to do so as well. Nowadays, perhaps more than ever before, professors, staff members, students, and even parents feel empowered to leap over several administrative layers in an attempt to get their way. Why follow the process when you can appeal directly to the provost or president? But violating protocol, or allowing others to do so, disrupts the orderly conduct of university business.

For example, you would not want to be blindsided by one of your faculty members who went directly to the dean to pitch a new program rather than starting with you as the department head. Similarly, if you were to take a departmental initiative first to the provost rather than to your dean, you would risk embarrassing the dean and perhaps losing his or her support.

Following protocol invariably works to your benefit. Maybe the timing is not right for your proposal, and the dean could potentially prevent you from making a strategic error in proposing the plan prematurely. Alternatively, your timing might be perfect, and the dean could be your best advocate. Either way, you win by working through proper channels.

In short, always keep your dean in the loop. And train faculty members in your department to follow basic protocol as well.

An effective department head works closely with the dean and the dean's staff members. The people in the dean's office are there to help you be successful as a chair and should be seen as your greatest support network. Don't isolate yourself and feel that you have to solve every problem on your own: "I don't want to trouble the dean with this one." Most deans would rather be "bothered" early, before a minor brush fire mushrooms into a major conflagration.

A key skill of a good department head is the ability to reserve judgment in a dispute until all parties have weighed in. Everyone who appeals for your support has a compelling story. Unsophisticated administrators assume that the first story they hear is the truth, or that the prevailing narrative about someone or some incident is accurate. Sophisticated administrators wait patiently to hear all sides before arriving at an opinion or rendering a verdict.

As the department's chief administrator, you are expected to maintain the highest standards of ethical behavior. No matter how close you are to certain colleagues in the department, you must do all that you can to avoid showing favoritism when evaluating faculty and staff members, making recommendations about raises, or scheduling courses.

The best department heads develop a healthy balance among their teaching, research, and administrative responsibilities. As the chief academic officer of your department, you should serve as a role model to your faculty—by being a lauded teacher, an active scholar, and a skilled administrator.

Sure, that balance is difficult to effect, and you are not going to have the time to devote to your teaching and research that you used to have. But keeping up your own work as much as possible is an important way to build credibility within the department and beyond.

One department head in my own college consistently teaches more courses than he is required to and recently won a universitywide award for outstanding teaching. Another chair regularly assigns himself huge lecture courses enrolling hundreds of students so he can justify providing course releases to active researchers. A third has garnered global attention for his research, including television documentaries and a lengthy story in *The New Yorker*.

All three have found a way to balance their many duties and to gain the respect of colleagues in the process.

That said, it is important that you not subordinate the management of your department to your teaching or research. Stories abound of department heads who have neglected the nuts and bolts of administration to concentrate on their own scholarship. Balance is the watchword.

Not everything we talked about at our panel will apply in every institutional context. Practices and campus cultures vary, but the issues I summarized here are ones that every chair will face on a daily basis. The job of department head may well be the toughest in the university, but you can make that job considerably harder by ignoring this good advice.

How Not to Evaluate Your Department Head

Summer is the time of year when deans prepare annual-performance evaluations for their department heads. For most of us, the new fiscal year begins on July 1, so in the preceding months we ask professors and staff members to comment on their department chairs.

Many institutions survey employees anonymously, asking them to answer a combination of multiple-choice and open-ended questions about their supervisors. Deans then analyze the survey data and use it to write the formal evaluations. (Some institutions ask faculty members to evaluate the deans and presidents, too.)

Reading this year's surveys of department chairs and school directors caused me to reflect on how flawed the typical evaluation process is in most institutions. Every year, I am shocked anew by both the statistically low participation rate in the surveys and the high level of vitriol that often characterizes the prose comments that are submitted.

Deans at some universities report that participation in the annual evaluations can be as low as 15 percent of the faculty and staff, and typically hovers around 30 percent. Just about any dean in the country can relate stories of evaluations characterized by a shocking torrent of rage and invective, often in lengthy typed diatribes.

A dean of arts and sciences in New England once told me that she loses sleep over the sheer viciousness of some evaluation remarks. "The unrestrained cruelty and ferocity of the anonymous evaluation narratives would make you think they are about enemy soldiers in some far-off war and not a fellow colleague who just so happens also to be your department chair," she told me. "It's ridiculously over the top."

Another dean told me that he has had faculty members who used the annual-evaluation process to accuse their department heads of serious criminal behavior—always without a shred of evidence.

Here are three comments that are fairly representative of the genre, made about department heads at an institution other than my own. They've been slightly altered to protect anonymity.

- Smith "is a disaster as a chair. He simply doesn't have the intellect or ability to manage the department. Morale is the lowest it's been in years, and several of us are certain he's dipping into department funds for personal use. My 10-year-old could do a better job than this idiot."

- Jones "is a liar and a drunk. He promises to get faculty input on important decisions but then does whatever he wants. You can usually smell the booze on him before noon. The dean should fire this sorry excuse for a human."

- Doe "is the worst chair in the department's history. Her communication skills are nonexistent. Half the time, she can't even produce a grammatical sentence. She's a disgrace to our department."

While those responses are clearly harsh, they aren't the nastiest I've seen. I've read some containing foul language, racial slurs, and other forms of hate speech.

The other issue, of course, is why so many faculty and staff members fail to participate at all in evaluating administrators.

One reason is that the evaluation process occurs at the worst time of the year for professors, who are busy grading final exams, commenting on seminar papers, preparing for commencement, and finalizing summer-travel plans. Completing an evaluation survey is one more task on an already full plate.

Also, much like voting patterns in our national elections, participation seems lowest when things are going well. When people are satisfied with their departments, they tend to direct their attention to more pressing concerns; when they are dissatisfied, they turn out in record numbers. Serious concern about the chair's performance will catapult the evaluation process to priority status for employees, but otherwise, it is likely to remain a low priority.

That dynamic can pervert the evaluation process. Here's a scenario that happens all too frequently: An effective and popular chairwoman has led her department to tranquillity and prosperity but, nonetheless, has angered a small number of faculty members over certain controversial decisions. She receives a statistically damning evaluation because the majority of professors are so content that they choose not to participate in the evaluation survey while the minority seize the initiative to condemn the chair.

By choosing not to participate, faculty members often work against their own best interests, potentially allowing a perspective they do not agree with to carry more weight than it should. What's more, a low turnout helps to erode an important element of shared governance that should be taken seriously by all parties.

Low participation is easy to explain, but it is less apparent why some faculty members feel compelled to submit anonymous narratives so hateful that they keep deans (and, undoubtedly, their department heads) from a restful sleep. An official evaluation process conducted in a professional setting calls for a "professional" response—that is, one that is factual and thoughtfully crafted, not characterized by emotional tirades, inappropriate language, gossip, or ad hominem attacks.

Besides, a long and angry diatribe is a sure way to undermine the credibility of your critique. An over-the-top response suggests (at least to many readers) that the writer has an ax to grind, or—in the most extreme cases—is perhaps unstable.

One dean I know refuses to read evaluation responses that are longer than a few paragraphs. "If there is that much seriously wrong with the chair," he explained to me, "the author should not have waited all year to bring it to my attention and to do so shielded by anonymity."

Inappropriate language also undercuts the credibility of your response and signals that the statement may say more about you than about the supervisor you are evaluating. That is not to deny people's passion—positive or negative—about their department heads; it is to say that the formal-evaluation process is not the most appropriate forum for such displays.

Those of us who rely on surveys in preparing performance evaluations must be especially skilled readers of those texts.

We need to be able to set aside excessive verbiage, emotional displays, recriminations, and rumor in order to extract the specific information that speaks most directly and reliably to the chair's performance. We should never assume that any given version of "the truth" is entirely reliable.

For those of you who take the time to answer open-ended survey questions about your department heads, here are a few suggestions that will ensure we take your response seriously:

- Keep it short. Long-winded statements undermine your credibility.

- Keep it factual. As with an effective letter of recommendation, the facts are what carry the day—not the adjectives, embellishments, and opinions. The dean or other supervisor reading your comments needs precise details illustrating your point, not an interpretation of what the details mean.

- Avoid displays of emotion. They are out of place in a professional setting and lead us to question your motives.

- Avoid recriminations, gossip, and accusations unfounded in any direct observation on your part.

- Above all, participate! Failing to register your opinion about an administrator's performance is a sure way to leave your dean with an incomplete or skewed picture.

To be clear, I am not suggesting you avoid submitting a substantive response, only that you keep it specific and succinct. Nor am I suggesting that you avoid criticism, only that the criticism be precise and factual. Content is important but so are tone and form.

Faculty members like to say they value shared governance. A central element of that is the annual evaluation of administrators, and it behooves us all to take the process seriously.

❖ ❖ ❖

Investigate Me, *Please*

Anyone who works in campus administration is used to internal audits. On several occasions, offices I have headed have been audited, and even more often I have ordered audits or investigations of departments that report to me. I have noticed over the years that many people become flustered and uptight about a scheduled audit, and that when they finally face the auditor they become noticeably tense, anxious, and uneasy.

"It's like when you're driving and suddenly look in your rearview mirror and discover that a cop is following you," one university auditor told me. "Even though you are perfectly innocent of any traffic violations, you become nervous and perhaps even a little paranoid. You slow down well below the speed limit and drive a little too carefully."

Some of us may well respond anxiously to university auditors, but they are not really internal law-enforcement officers. In fact, an auditor can be an administrator's best friend. I know some administrators who typically ask that their department be audited whenever they accept a new appointment, because they want to begin their new position fully aware of any risks or concerns.

Perhaps knowing a bit about the craft of auditing will help us to approach university auditors not as enforcers and adversaries but as colleagues and allies who potentially can save us from embarrassment—or worse.

Rather than focusing on ensnaring someone, the auditor's true mission is to protect the institution from risk, all kinds of risk. Is the department (or official) exposing the institution to a lawsuit? Or a fine from a regulatory body? Or liability resulting from a safety hazard? Or the likelihood of fraud or some future infraction because there are insufficient internal controls to prevent it? (An internal control is a policy or procedure established to prevent violations, as when a policy dictates that more than one official be required to sign a form in order for someone to access university money from an account.)

Auditors are valuable to institutions because they provide an independent perspective on a department. If an office is out of compliance, especially with state or federal regulations, it is much preferable to learn about that internally, so that the problems can be corrected, than to have an external agency discover the violations. One lawsuit or federal fine could cost an institution millions of dollars, so preventing or minimizing risk is a valuable exercise.

Most auditors perform several kinds of reviews, but the two most common are audits and investigations. An audit is a planned activity, usually conducted on a regular basis—perhaps every few years—although "special audits" can also be requested at any time. An investigation is an effort to discover whether something has occurred: a law broken, a regulation ignored, a rule violated. An investigation is narrower in scope than an audit, and is usually initiated by an allegation.

An auditor may begin an audit interview by asking a department head to identify the top three potential risks and then ask what steps have been taken to mitigate them. The reviewer might then ask, "What type of monitoring do you have in place to ensure that those risks are properly managed?"

The reviewer might eventually ask, "Are there any activities your department performs that could lead to adverse publicity because of the nature of your operations?" Examples might include hazardous-waste disposal or research involving controlled substances or human or animal subjects. Just as a violation of rules or laws can expose the institution to risk, so, can adverse publicity if something were to go awry. It's much better to identify, assess, and manage the risks in advance than to be blindsided later.

Auditors are likely to inquire whether your department has experienced a change in key personnel over the past year and whether procedures are clearly documented so that successors can continue their duties without a major disruption. That question is meant to determine whether you have taken appropriate measures to cross-train essential staff members. Otherwise you have placed the institution at risk were you suddenly to lose an indispensable employee.

A typical area that all auditors will examine is whether any conflicts of interest exist in a department. Has the chair hired his daughter's restaurant to cater all department functions? Has the supervisor accepted any "gifts" from a provider who hopes to sign a contract with the department? In short, are there any circumstances in which an accountable officer has the opportunity to obtain personal gain from an official decision that only he or she makes? Those are the kinds of areas of risk that auditors are trained to ferret out.

University auditors also perform focused investigations, usually of specific people: A faculty member is accused of charging a vacation trip to a grant account, a department chair is alleged to have misappropriated department money for personal use, a staff member is said to have engaged in petty theft, a dean is accused of "cooking the books."

Unlike audits, which are usually broad probes into the practices of a department, investigations are meant to determine if a specific person (or group of people) has engaged in an inappropriate act. But even in formal investigations, the role of the auditor is to determine the facts in a case, not to determine guilt or innocence. The appropriate administrator will do that based on the auditor's report.

Over the years, the role of university auditor has become increasingly professionalized. Auditors today must undergo substantial training. Many are certified public accountants. Others are certified internal auditors, and still others are certified fraud examiners. Some have all three types of training. Those specialists are supported by a number of national professional groups, including the Association of College & University Auditors, the Institute of Internal Auditors, and the Association of Certified Fraud Examiners.

University auditors may make us uncomfortable as they ask us the tough questions that we should be asking ourselves, but their role is not to trap us; it is to protect us and the institution.

One auditor I know said that good auditors do not approach clients with suspicion. He has adopted the familiar Reagan-era phrase as his office's motto: "Trust but verify."

"Our job is simply to find the facts," he told me—a goal that auditors share with all of us in academe.

Safety First

A respected nuclear physicist mistakenly allows his graduate assistant to run a workshop at the university's small-scale version of a nuclear reactor and exposes the class to radiation. At another institution, a fume hood fails to contain an acrid gas in a chemistry laboratory, causing several students to be rushed to the hospital.

With so many potential risks of serious health-and-safety problems at colleges and universities, you'd think that safety officers would be among the best-known administrators on any campus. Yet they have one of those jobs in higher education that tends to be invisible, much like auditors or institutional researchers: Everyone knows they're important, but no one quite understands what they do.

In another column, I explored the role of the college auditor. Many readers wrote to thank me for demystifying the craft and showing how an auditor's job is to protect not only the institution but also those who work there. So I'd like to take the same approach to health-and-safety officers.

The sheer number of risks to health and safety—especially at research universities—is considerable. That's why most institutions support a health-and-safety officer, and often an entire office of them. The position has become indispensable, no matter that many people on campus are unaware of the safety officer's existence.

Safety offices are variously named and have missions specific to their institutions. At the University of South Florida, the division of environmental health and safety provides "education, hazard assessment, exposure mitigation, and the responsible management of hazardous materials." At Iowa State University, the department of environmental health and safety seeks to protect employees and the public from "chemical, microbiological and physical health hazards. . . . These factors may be present as a result of workplace activities, ineffective building systems, or environmental influences."

On my own campus, Idaho State University, we have a technical safety office. Because Idaho State offers programs in nuclear engineering, health physics, and the health sciences, it is no surprise that the safety office's mission is "to ensure that radiation and radioactivity, lasers, and hazardous and biomedical wastes at ISU are managed safely and in accordance with applicable federal and state laws and regulations."

The overriding objective of any university safety office is twofold: to protect people from harm, and to protect the institution from liability. The most successful safety officer is one who continually focuses on accident prevention and regulatory compliance rather than on reacting to safety crises.

The typical safety office will monitor biohazards produced from research on, say, a virulent virus or bacterium. It will oversee appropriate disposal of hazardous waste, chemical-spill response protocols, and Environmental Protection Agency compliance and reporting. And, of course, it will coordinate with the Department of Homeland Security when the university handles substances that are high security.

A full-service safety office, however, monitors much more than exotic hazards. It will also be concerned with such risks as asbestos exposure, asthma triggers in the workplace (bacteria, mold, and fungi associated with sick-building syndrome), fire hazards, indoor air pollution, and machine-shop safety.

Sometimes the problems are far more mundane. One safety officer told me that his "biggest headache" is controlling potential accidents caused by departmental or personal negligence, such as "storing" items in public hallways adjacent to faculty offices.

"It's amazing how many fire and safety hazards faculty and staff will create if left unchecked," he said. "I've seen file cabinets and unwanted desks shoved out into hallways, boxes of books stacked five high, and even people's personal refrigerators and hot plates set up in the hallway as if this public space were an extension of their office."

Another safety officer told me that he himself was injured when he tripped on the power cord of a faculty member's refrigerator, which was located in the hallway just outside a research laboratory.

"It was a bit embarrassing," he said. "Here I was, the university's safety officer, in the process of investigating potential safety risks, and I myself became victim to one."

Asked to name the problems he and his colleagues most commonly face, a safety officer gave me this list:

- **Extension cords.** That includes using cords of insufficient thickness to handle the power requirements of the devices being used; running cords under doors, particularly if they are pinched when the door opens or closes; and failing to replace a frayed or otherwise damaged cord.

- **Bookcases.** The big problem here is failing to secure bookcases to a wall when they are more than four feet tall. A colleague was permanently injured when a bookcase tipped over and fell on him in a freak accident.

- **Clutter.** Creating tripping hazards of any sort, or any clutter that can prevent rapid egress in the event of an emergency.

- **Chairs.** Tilting back in a four-legged chair so that only two of the legs are touching the ground has caused a surprisingly large number of office accidents. The motto here should be, "Keep six feet on the ground!"

- **Improper storage.** You're asking for trouble if you store combustibles under staircases, in stairwells, in hallways, or too close to the ceiling.

- **Unrated ladders.** University employees should obtain equipment approved by the National Institute for Occupational Safety and Health. Fiberglass ladders, not aluminum, are usually recommended, especially since they are not conductors of electricity.

- **Hoarding.** Storing excessive amounts of belongings in an office is both a fire hazard and a potential obstacle to egress. I have had several colleagues over the years whose offices were so excessively cramped with books and stacks of papers that one was tempted to wonder if this were not a manifestation of some underlying mental-health problem.

If your research involves specific safety issues such as nuclear waste or biohazards, then you will need to follow the appropriate guidelines and regulations. But the rest of us, too, can take steps to improve the safety climate on our campuses.

So don't rig wiring. Don't keep a hot plate inches away from a large stack of papers. Immediately report an acrid or unusual odor. Don't exceed the fire code's maximum capacity of a classroom by moving in extra desks. And when in doubt, check with the campus safety officer.

Index